Penguin Ha

Danish Coo

Nika Hazelto
and England. ...
Harper's Bazaar and other magazines in the United States, which is now her permanent home except for trips. In the past she has also worked as an advertising copywriter, but now she is a freelance contributor to *House and Garden*, *Town and Country*, the American *National Review* and several other periodicals. Among her books are *Reminiscence and Ravioli*, *The Art of Cheese Cookery*, *The Continental Flavour*, *The Art of Scandinavian Cooking*, *The Best of Italian Cooking*, *The Swiss Cookbook* and *The Belgian Cookbook*. She loves to travel to different and exotic places – such as Lapland at Christmas-time. She adores both the Arctic North and the Mediterranean.

Nika Hazelton

DANISH COOKING

Penguin Books

Penguin Books Ltd, Harmondsworth,
Middlesex, England
Penguin Books Australia Ltd, Ringwood,
Victoria, Australia

First published in the U.S.A. by Doubleday 1964
Published, with revisions, in Penguin Books 1967
Reprinted 1974

Made and printed in Great Britain by
Cox & Wyman Ltd, London, Reading and Fakenham
Set in Monotype Baskerville

Contents

Recipes for items marked with an asterisk may be located by consulting the Index.

Acknowledgements

My gratitude and thanks go to the many Danish people whose generosity and patience made this book possible. I wish I could mention them all by name.

My very special thanks to Mrs A. W. Nielsen, the wife of the director of the Carlsberg Breweries, and Mrs Rosalie Holmes of the Federation of Danish Dairy Associations, for all their help and, more important still, their friendship.

NIKA HAZELTON

About the Recipes

All the recipes in this book are authentically Danish and the fruit of long stays in Denmark, among Danish people. Danish food is wonderful, but it would have been impossible to include all of it in one book. I had to settle for the dishes that I consider the most typical of Danish cooking, and I beg the indulgence of the readers who may miss some of their favourites.

Originally, this book was written for American cooks. Since some American and English culinary terms are different, the publishers and I have done our best to use the terms familiar to English cooks in this edition. However, American versus English cooking language was not the main bother. There is a much more important, indeed, a truly basic difference between the cookbooks of the two countries, and that is in the way the recipes are written. This difference stems from the cooking habits of the two countries.

In one sentence: American cooks measure all of their ingredients, such as flour, butter, milk, etc., whereas British cooks weigh the solid ones. In the United States, few cooks have kitchen scales, but no cook is without two sets of utterly standardized kitchen equipment made from heatproof glass, aluminium or other metals. One set consists of 1 cup, ½ cup, ⅓ cup and ¼ cup. The other consists of 1 tablespoon, 1 teaspoon, ½ teaspoon and ¼ teaspoon. These are the measures an American cook will use when she reads: 'Take 1 cup flour, ½ cup water and ½ teaspoon salt.'

As far as possible English equivalents in ounces and pints have been substituted in the recipes. These equivalents might not be accepted by a Standards Board, but neither would be the majority of the kitchen scales in use. But you can cook from them.

Some recipes still contain cup measurements. *The American standard cup holds 8 fluid ounces, whereas the British standard cup holds 10 fluid ounces.* The American cup is obtainable at large stores in this country. An alternative method is to find a large cup, small basin or other receptacle which holds exactly 8 fluid ounces, and keep it for use with this book.

In any case, almost all cooking needs some adapting. Most cooks do this automatically, adding a little more liquid to dilute to a proper consistency, or thickening with flour or increasing or decreasing the sugar in a pudding. This adapting does not affect many main dishes, such as soups, stews, roasts, and gravies, but it does affect baking, which is a chemical process (like all cooking) that is based upon an exact relation between the various ingredients which must be followed accurately. Here cooks will have to do a little experimenting in their Danish baking to achieve perfect results, and at least the conversion tables will give a reasonable guide as to quantities.

Another point that comes up in this discussion is that the recipes in this book were not only tested with American kitchen equipment, but with American foods as well. Some of these also vary from their English counterparts. The butterfat in English cream is different from that in American cream, English plain flour absorbs liquids somewhat differently from American all-purpose flour, and American 'cake' flour is something else again, since it is made from soft rather than hard wheat. Meat cuts are also different, and this will affect their cooking times. Here again, the cook will soon learn to be guided by her own experience.

Unless indicated differently, the recipes in this book will give approximately 4 to 6 servings.

Weights and Measures

AMERICAN	ENGLISH
¼ cup – 2 fl. oz.	$\frac{1}{10}$ pint
½ cup – 4 fl. oz.	⅕ pint
1 cup – 8 fl. oz.	⅖ pint
2 cups – 16 fl. oz.	⅘ pint
4 cups – 32 fl. oz.	1⅗ pint

MOST COMMON DRY MEASURES

Butter, solid fats, solidly packed	
2 tablespoons	1 oz.
¼ cup – 4 tablespoons	2 oz.
½ cup – 8 tablespoons	¼ lb.
1 cup – 16 tablespoons	½ lb.
2 cups	1 lb.
Sugar	
¼ cup – 4 tablespoons	2 oz.
½ cup – 8 tablespoons	¼ lb.
1 cup plus 3 tablespoons	½ lb.
2⅓ cups	1 lb.
Flour, sifted	
1 tablespoon	¼ oz.
¼ cup – 4 tablespoons	1 oz.
½ cup – 8 tablespoons	2 oz.
1 cup plus 4 tablespoons	¼ lb.
4½ cups	1 lb.

1 cup apple sauce about 9 oz.
1 cup diced apple about 4⅓ oz.
1 cup sliced beetroot about 6 oz.
1 cup cubed cheese about 4 oz.
1 cup blue cheese about 4 oz.
1 cup dry grated cheese about 4 oz.
1 cup diced cucumber about 4 to 5 oz.

1 cup currants about 5 oz.
1 cup chopped dill about 2 to 3 oz.
1 cup grapes about 6 oz.
1 cup diced ham about 5 oz.
1 cup raw minced meat about 8 oz.
1 cup cubed raw meat about 8 oz.
1 cup cubed cooked meat about 5 oz.
1 cup uncooked oatmeal about $2\frac{3}{4}$ oz.
1 cup cooked oatmeal about $9\frac{1}{2}$ oz.
1 cup chopped onion about $4\frac{3}{4}$ oz.
1 cup chopped or minced parsley about 2 to 3 oz.
1 cup peas about $5\frac{3}{4}$ oz.
1 cup mashed potato about $7\frac{1}{3}$ oz.
1 cup diced potatoes about $5\frac{3}{4}$ oz.
1 cup chopped prawns about 6 to 8 oz.
1 cup whole prawns about 4 oz.
1 cup chopped uncooked prunes about $5\frac{3}{4}$ oz.
1 cup chopped cooked prunes about $9\frac{1}{2}$ oz.
1 cup sour pickles about 8 oz.
1 cup raisins about $5\frac{1}{4}$ oz.
1 cup raspberries about 2 oz.
1 cup red currant jelly about 10 oz.
1 cup uncooked rice about 8 oz.
1 cup drained tomatoes about 6 oz.
1 cup chopped vegetables about 5 oz.

Oven Temperatures

ELECTRICITY		GAS
Very slow	250 – 275° F.	½ – 1
Slow	300 – 325° F.	2 – 3
Moderate	350 – 375° F.	4 – 5
Hot	400 – 425° F.	6 – 7
Very hot	450 – 475° F.	8 – 9
Extremely hot	475 – 525° F.	9 – 10

Introduction

Denmark is ravishing. The little kingdom, about half the size of Scotland and with a population of about four and a half million people, is all sparkling blue waters surrounding the five hundred-odd Danish isles, fairy-tale little towns, crenelated castles mirrored in their moats, and whitewashed, often thatched farms set in fields that look like well tended gardens. The capital, Copenhagen, is an architectural delight and one of the best cities in Europe for pleasure walks. It is also the gayest after-dark capital in Europe, after Paris.

The Danes themselves are a friendly, hospitable, and generous people, and they laugh at pretty much the same things we do. Practically all the Danes speak English, which is mandatory in the schools. They are hard-working and thrifty, but in Denmark there's nothing glum about these virtues. On the contrary. The Danes are anything but puritanical; they enjoy life from every angle. And they have marvellous food, both at home and in the restaurants that for haute cuisine, decorative presentation, and flawless service rank with the best in Europe.

One of the reasons why a visit to Denmark is most rewarding is that the country is so small that even a foreigner can see and understand a lot in a little time, since the travelling is easy and well organized. It's also extremely pleasant for a visitor to be in a country that is scrupulously honest in all dealings, as well as spotlessly clean. I've seen well-dressed men pick up a bit of stray paper in the street and drop it in the nearest wastepaper basket, shaking their heads in sorrow that paper should be lying in the street in the first place.

Denmark is a constitutional monarchy, and the royal family is treated by the Danes with much deep affection and pride, without any maudlin mystique. The government is democratically elected. The standard of living is high, and expressed in the saying: 'Few have too much or too little.' The country has admirable social services far superior to the

English ones. The Danish language is different from English and other European languages, but sufficiently similar to Norwegian and Swedish to make it possible for Scandinavians to understand each other while they talk in their own language.

Nowhere is food more plentiful and more beautifully served than in Denmark. And nowhere is good food more enjoyed and taken for granted. The Danes like to eat well and often, and to talk about food. Where we, after a party, will ask: 'Did you have a good time?' the Danes will want to know: 'What did you have to eat?' expecting and getting a full answer.

Danish Food

Everyday family food, in Denmark, is a very different proposition from party and restaurant food. The first is simple and thrifty, though tasty, the second, of an opulence and presentation the likes of which we have not seen since the days of Edward VII.

The Danish foods best known outside the country are smørrebrød, open-faced sandwiches consisting of slices of thickly buttered bread topped with anything from a slice of cold pork to an arrangement of fish or meat, salad, aspic and decorations of tomato slices, eggs, pickles, radish roses, and lemon twists and Danish pastries. Denmark's Danish pastries are very rich, and delicious.

Danish family food includes simple open-faced sandwiches, cod, herring, haddock, and plaice, a profusion of cured pork and some fresh roast pork, sausage, beef and veal used economically in ground or minced form, a few vegetables and salads, and simple puddings and cakes. Party and restaurant food goes in for elaborate smørrebrød, lobster, the infinitesimal and exquisite Danish shrimp, trout, salmon, turbot, roast beef, roast veal, roast lamb, roast duck and goose, venison, and game birds.

With some exceptions, the relation between Danes and vegetables and salads is a tenuous one. Family vegetables are cabbage, red cabbage, carrots, knob celery or celeriac, and canned peas, as well as fresh peas, string beans, and other summer vegetables. Festive vegetables are asparagus, thick, snow white, tender, and wonderful even when canned, and the superlative Danish mushrooms, which a Danish hostess puts into the gravy or serves creamed when she wants to honour a guest.

As for salads, the tossed green salad is known only to sophisticates. To the ordinary Dane, a salad is a dish composed of several vegetables and possibly even fish or meat, bound with mayonnaise or another creamy dressing often used as a smørrebrød topping. Lettuce and tomatoes are used a great deal, but as edible decorations. On the other hand, cucumbers pickled with vinegar and sugar, a refreshing and crisp way of preparing them, and pickled beets are eaten constantly as accompaniments to fish and flesh.

The Danes look upon eggs as an ingredient rather than a dish *per se*, with the exception of boiled breakfast eggs and a kind of flat omelet made with bacon. And the more eggs are put into a cake or a cream, the better it will be. The superb Danish cheese is eaten on smørrebrød, or with fruit for dessert, but seldom cooked with.

As for desserts, all Danes have a sweet tooth, or perhaps two. Family desserts are stewed fruits thickened with a little cornflour and served with cream, pancakes, sweet soups made with fruit, and simple cakes eaten with coffee, after the meal. Party desserts are luscious beyond belief, creations fashioned with fruits, almond paste, rich layer cakes with even richer fillings, meringues, served preferably with billows of whipped cream. These incredible Danish fancy desserts are embellished like an eighteenth-century lady-in-waiting out to tempt the King. They tempt the diner beyond endurance, and he yields with a 'never mind, never mind' as he takes his shameless third helping.

The glories of Danish baking are Danish pastries, made from one basic recipe, the crisp layer cakes filled with assorted creams, *sandkage*, a rich, plain cake, and *kransekage*, which consists almost entirely of almond paste. Almonds are the leitmotiv of Danish baking, and most of the cookies that are baked *en masse* around Christmas are rich with them. Pastry shops, called *konditorier*, abound, and they are filled with Danes and foreigners alike who cannot resist the dozens of rich, luscious, and beautifully decorated cakes. But Danish women still bake a great deal at home, and it is expected of them. A Danish hostess will tell you, 'I have baked a little something for you,' as she sits you down to a beautifully appointed coffee table with several cakes and three kinds of cookies.

Beer is the national Danish drink, and so is akvavit, a fiery spirit distilled from barley or potatoes and served ice-cold with smørrebrød. Coffee, good, strong, and hot, is drunk the clock round. And a surprising amount of soda pop is consumed by the Danish young.

How Danish food differs from ours

All in all, Danish food is much richer than English food; it is also much blander, traditionally. Even the curried dishes – and curry is the one exotic spice Danes like – are very mild. The Danish taste for sharper, spicier foods is gratified in the smørrebrød toppings, the endless variety of pickled herrings and other fish, the smoked eel, the piquant salads, and in the national passion for horse-radish and mustard.

The Danes are also conservative in their food habits, and they don't mind eating the same dishes day in, day out. In Copenhagen, city of superb restaurants, there are very few that are not Danish, though these will serve French-inspired dishes. Where Danish dishes are very different from ours is in the way they combine foods. Beef stew comes with bacon curls, kidneys with sausage, boiled chicken with shrimp and asparagus, and vegetables are also often included in these one-dish combinations.

What's surprising to the non-Scandinavian visitor is the Danish love for sauces and for potatoes. The main one is brown sauce, with plain and fancy variations such as onion or madeira. White sauce and its offspring come second, and they are often enriched with whipped cream, and flavoured with mustard or horse-radish. Melted butter is also very popular, especially with fish. There is hardly a dish that is not served with a sauce, and after a spell of Danish eating you begin to wonder if the Danes think it indecent for a dish to come to the table uncloaked with a rich and often splendid sauce.

The reason that so many sauces are used is probably the fact that practically all fish and meat dishes are served with boiled potatoes or, in second place, with potatoes browned with sugar and butter. Potato chips are the next favourite, and ordinary Danish cooking seldom goes beyond these three ways of serving potatoes. So great is the Danish love for potatoes that not only are they served at every meal but sometimes, as an accompaniment to meats, you even get two kinds of potatoes, such as boiled and browned, or browned and chips. But it is the boiled potato that is triumphant, and to deprive a Dane of his boiled potatoes would be as cruel as depriving a baby of his bottle. However, Danish potatoes are delicious, and much more flavoured than English ones. They are also grown in far more varieties, and selected carefully by the housewives, rather than bought in an offhand manner, as in America or in England.

Except for dried yellow peas, which are the base for *gule aerter*, the national soup, the Danes don't use beans or legumes; and they use little macaroni or rice. In cooking and baking, they use margarine to a great extent. It is very good, but nothing beats Denmark's golden butter except the best fresh English farm butter.

Changing Danish food habits

Danish food habits were set by history and geography. While the peasants and artisans ate the filling dishes of the labouring classes – the barley, oats, and other porridges and gruels, the pork they raised and cured themselves, the herring, fresh and salted, the cabbage, and above all the potatoes – the food of the middle classes and of the aristocracy was strongly influenced by that of the Danish court. Denmark was an absolute monarchy from 1660 to 1849, and the Danish court the sun that nourished the nobles, whose castles and manor houses are among the delights of Danish architecture. Like all European courts, the Danish one was strongly influenced by France, and Danish food by baroque and rococo cooking of the seventeenth and eighteenth centuries. In their turn, the well-to-do merchants and traders of the rising Danish middle class copied the aristocracy, only to be copied themselves by those below them. Thus the recipes from the Danish castles and manor houses trickled down to farm and cottage, setting the pattern for Danish cooking.

To this day the Danes will point out with pride that their cooking is French. Indeed, it is influenced by the French cooking of the Golden Age, and embellished and enrichened in a way no longer current in France. And everyday food, especially on the farms, is still plain and simple, echoing the old days.

But Danish food habits are changing very rapidly, thanks to modern food processing and modern transportation. The Danes are a practical people, and if something is really convenient, such as canned foods, they will adopt it without further ado. Frozen foods, including many varieties of vegetables not used before, such as broccoli, are gaining rapid acceptance. Modern communications have brought not only out-of-season treats such as lettuce from Italy and vegetables from France at times when none grow in Denmark, but also a knowledge of how other nations eat. The Danes are great travellers, and though conservative, they are slowly beginning to take to lighter and more varied foods. The women's magazines have devoted themselves to putting Danish eating on a better balanced and more rational basis. The Danish government, too, has an admirable food programme through its extension services and its school home economics classes, which are mandatory. Thus Danish eating is in many ways far more modern than you would think from some of the standard Danish cookbooks. And foreigners, when they see the lavishness of restaurant food and the Danes' enjoyment of it, should remember that daily eating is very plain and moderate – the reason for feasting when eating out.

Danish mealtimes

The Danes eat a light breakfast of coffee, several kinds of light and dark bread served with generous amounts of butter and jam, and perhaps a boiled egg and a bit of cheese. Denmark is largely an agricultural country, the big English breakfast of bacon and eggs, fish, or meats is not known; the Danish farmer will content himself with porridge.

Lunch is around noon, and it consists of smørrebrød, plain or fancy. If eaten in a restaurant, or when there are visitors, a hot dish may follow the open-faced sandwiches.

Coffee-cum-cake parties are held during the afternoon by the women; in the cities, they may meet for a cup of tea at one of the cafés and treat themselves to the irresistible pastries.

Dinner, interestingly called *middag*, or midday, is eaten early, around six or so. A family will have perhaps soup and pancakes, or fish and boiled potatoes, or a dish of minced meat with boiled potatoes and cucumber salad. A simple fruit dessert may round off the meal. After dinner the Danes go out – in Copenhagen, it seems the whole population is abroad. They go to the cafés, the movies, dancing, or just out for a beer. From nine o'clock on they eat again, usually more smørrebrød, and perhaps a little cake or cookies. If a party goes on late, food will be served again later, along the same lines, to sustain life until breakfast.

Smørrebrød and the Cold Table

Roast Lamb and Cucumber Salad
Roast Pork and Beetroot
Tongue and Horse-radish
Bacon, Onion, and Apples
Bacon and Mushrooms
Hard-boiled Eggs and Russian Herring Salad or Italian Salad
Liver Paste with Beetroot
Frikadeller (Danish Meat Balls) with Cucumber Salad
Smoked Eel
Roast Chicken
Chicken Salad
Camembert
Cucumber Blue Cheese
Ham and Chicken
Ham and Egg

FESTIVE SMØRREBRØD

Shrimp
Beef Tartare
Smoked Salmon with Spinach and Mushroom Caps
Ham and Chicken Salad
Goose Liver Pâté with Ham and Madeira
Danish Blue Cheese and Egg
Fried Fish Fillets with Remoulade Sauce
Hans Christian Andersen's Sandwich
Liver Pâté and Tongue
The Vet's Midnight Supper
Lobster
Marrow
Scrambled Egg with Mussels and Spinach
Meat Salad
Cod or Shad Roe Salad

MEATS, SALADS, AND OTHER SMØRREBRØD TOPPINGS AND KOLDT BORD DISHES

Duck or Goose Dripping
Spiced Pork Fat

WARM SMØRREBRØD

Of Smørrebrød and the Cold Table

Danish sandwiches are a food category in themselves. They are open-faced, eaten with a fork and knife, and they come in hundreds of varieties of fish, fowl, meat, eggs, aspics, vegetables, salads, cheese, and fruit combinations. Danish sandwiches are as colourful as a Persian tapestry and as artfully designed for visual appeal as a show window. They are delicious, easy and amusing to make, and very well suited to modern English life because in a quick, practical, and thrifty way they introduce a powerful amount of variety into daily food. A Danish open-faced sandwich is almost a meal in itself, but it can also be cut in two to make a *snitter* or slicelet, or further reduced in size to make delightful appetizers and hors d'oeuvres for a party.

Small sandwiches, judiciously composed to match flavour and appearance and dished up prettily, can make a hostess's reputation. Larger in size, they can be served as late evening refreshments, along with a glass of Danish Carlsberg or Tuborg beer, in the Danish manner. They do not need very elaborate toppings, as long as they look colourful and the combination of foods is appetizing.

The Danish name for their sandwiches is smørrebrød, meaning literally butter (smørre) and bread (brød). And bread and butter is the foundation on which all Danish sandwiches are built, whether they consist of a slice of cold roast pork with a few pickle slices or a 'high' sandwich made with a freshly fried fillet of fish, asparagus, prawns, and salmon and decorated with pieces of lobster, sautéed mushrooms, and a twist of lemon.

Smørrebrød is Denmark's national dish, and every Dane, man, woman, and child, eats smørrebrød for lunch, at home, in restaurants, at a desk in the office, by the workbench, or in school. A housewife will put up smørrebrød for her family, packing it in specially constructed metal or plastic cases designed to prevent the topping from being squashed, and make herself a few slices from yesterday's left-overs, which she'll eat in the kitchen, with a cup of coffee. An executive will eat his smørrebrød at his desk during the short Danish lunch hour, and should he go out to a restaurant, he'll also eat smørrebrød. A farmer will eat his smørrebrød at night. All Danes will have smørrebrød during the evening, at the end of a party, and whenever they feel the need for sustenance.

Hand in hand with smørrebrød goes the koldt bord or cold table, the elaborate Danish version of the Swedish smørgasbord. The cold table consists of the same foods that make the smørrebrød toppings, but they are arranged in dishes and on platters. You select your foods and make up your own smørrebrød by buttering a piece of bread with the marvellous Danish butter and topping it as you please. All in all, this is nothing but hors d'oeuvres eaten on buttered bread rather than in the French manner, but the hors d'oeuvres make the meal, though they might be followed with a 'little hot dish' (*småretter*) instead of being the introduction to a meal, as they are in France.

Creating smørrebrød and a cold table is a Danish national art. Let alone the yard-long menu of the sandwich specialist Oskar Davidsen in his Copenhagen restaurant, the smørrebrød menu of any good Danish restaurant must be seen to be believed. At the restaurant of the Hotel d'Angleterre in Copenhagen (a vast, carpeted, and supremely comfortable establishment in the most elegant continental manner, where you expect to find – and find – prime ministers, international financiers, and famous beauties) no less than 157 different ways of putting a topping on a slice of bread and butter are the order of the day. Thirty-four ways alone are devoted to arrangements with fresh and smoked meats; the rest are given to affairs using fresh, salted, and smoked fish, sausages, eggs, salads, vegetables, and cheese, and, no doubt for timid souls, ordinary English sandwiches with merely ham, chicken, or other standard ingredients. At the Rødvig Kro, a charming old country inn by the lapping waves of the Baltic, the luncheon guest, to get up his strength to consume the hot little dishes of his menu, is presented with a picturesque array of four different kinds of herring, curry salad, lobster salad, herring salad, Italian salad, prawns, plain and as a salad, tuna fish, cooked salt cod, sardines, smoked eel, smoked salmon, ham, tongue, cold roast pork, cold rib roast, cold roast beef, chicken, liver pâté, beef tartare, veal loaf, jellied ham, cold bacon, sausages, smoked pork, pork tenderloin, fresh and smoked, lamb chops, fried plaice, hard-boiled eggs, tomatoes, and various cheeses. Each dish of this cold table is decked out with lettuce leaves and garnished with tomato slices, radish roses, egg slices, cucumber and lemon twists, dill and parsley sprigs, pickles, and sprinkles of paprika wherever it looks good. The reaction of many a tender soul, seeing the beautiful sandwiches and cold board dishes, has been that the pride of Denmark is too beautiful to eat. But greed has always overcome sensitivity.

The tipple that goes with smørrebrød is of two kinds, involving the two basic national drinks, akvavit and beer.

Akvavit (the name means literally water of life) is called *snaps* in daily parlance, and it is a dry, very potent spirit with a vague caraway flavour. All Danish akvavit is made in Aalborg, a jolly town in North Jutland, famous for its splendidly decorated Renaissance mansions, an excellent opera, and for rejoicing in fine food. There the water of life is made from the very best and most scientifically produced grain or barley alcohol, for the goodness of akvavit depends on the spirits used. The process resembles that of making gin. Akvavit is part of Danish life, and Danish women put it away with the best and nary a stagger. A whole book could be filled with its lore, but suffice to quote a verse found on a *kluksflaske*, a special decanter that says *kluk-kluk* as you pour:

> Pure as a maiden and strong as her lover;
> Hot as the heart so ardently lit;
> Cool as the well where spring breezes hover.
> That – that, my friend, is en dansk akvavit.

The water of life is exported under the name AALBORG AKVAVIT with an alcoholic strength of 86 proof. I recommend it as a pre-dinner drink since it is pure, and also simple to serve. But it should be chilled in the refrigerator.

The second national drink is beer, practically all of which is made by two of the largest breweries in the world, Carlsberg and Tuborg. Danish beer is about the best in Europe, brewed from malts so special that they are exported even to Germany as the base for the famous German beers. Most of the beer drunk in Denmark is of the Pilsner kind, but there are many other varieties, such as, at one end, a powerful export brewed by Tuborg and, at the other, a low-alcohol Pilsner made by Carlsberg, with any number of stouts, sweet beers, and a dark, unsweetened ship's beer in between. Both Carlsberg and Tuborg are such stupendous institutions that no visitor should fail to visit them. A staggering amount of beer is brewed yearly – these two breweries each make more than 500 million bottles per year.

Smørrebrød, akvavit, and beer go far more closely with each other than love and marriage. The akvavit arrives at the table arctic cold, and usually embedded in a cylinder of ice. It is poured into thimble-sized glasses. With it comes your glass or bottle of beer. You eat a bite and follow with a sip or, if you're strong or Danish, with a full glass of akvavit. This, in turn, is followed immediately with a beer chaser. Thus the drink called boilermaker in America is in full swing at any Danish table.

As I said before, smørrebrød is a very good idea for English entertaining. Unless the sandwiches are prepared for a cocktail party, it is better to have the toppings arranged cold-table fashion if the smørrebrød is to be the main part of a meal. There should be a variety of breads and butter, in curls or balls or decorative pats, for the guest to choose from.

Each guest should have a stack of plates, one for each category of sandwiches, so as not to mix the flavours, and also several forks and knives, for the same reason. He starts helping himself to the fish dishes, proceeds to the meats and salads, and goes on, ending with a cheese smørrebrød. In Denmark the actual buttering of the bread and placing of the topping is done on a small teak board, which resembles a cutting-board. The plate is removed and the silver changed after each course, so to speak.

And of course each guest has his little akvavit glass in front of him, as well as a glass for his bottle of beer.

Smørrebrød Suggestions

Only an entire book devoted to smørrebrød and koldt bord could possibly do justice to all the delightful combinations one comes across in Denmark. These include not only the open-faced sandwiches eaten for lunch and for snacks, but their offspring, the cocktail canapés and appetizers, the sandwich rolls and appetizer tortes which are usually very elaborate affairs, decorated to the last inch, and the baked pastry shells, some tiny, some bigger, filled with succulent and diversified fillings. With the exception of the open-faced sandwiches, these goodies are not typically Danish, and practically all of them can be found in comprehensive English and French cookbooks, and in books devoted to cocktail foods, both hot and cold.

In Denmark there are shops where sandwich toppings are sold and where prepared smørrebrød can be bought. These shops are excellently patronized by Danish housewives. In England a trip to a delicatessen, especially one featuring Scandinavian foods, will yield a treasure of smørrebrød fixings, such as an infinite variety of canned herring, tiny Danish shrimps, Danish caviar, smoked eel, canned meats and sausages, pâtés, and cheeses. What also helps is a look into the refrigerator and the store cupboard, for smørrebrød of the everyday variety is also the Danish way of using left-overs in a pleasant, fanciful, and very tasty manner. As for the smørrebrød that consists of a number of cooked ingredients, such as roast chicken with creamed mushrooms, or ham and spinach, or fried fish with prawns. I have always thought of it as the Danish way of serving related foods. We do it on a plate, they do it on a slice of buttered bread, using smaller quantities. Thinking of smørrebrød this way will help you to compose interesting varieties. And serve your smørrebrød Danish style with ice-cold Aalborg akvavit and a bottle of Danish beer.

Here are some hints to help you make good smørrebrød.

Freshness

Danish sandwiches taste best when fresh, and therefore they should be assembled as close to serving time as possible. The bread, however, may be buttered beforehand and kept covered in the refrigerator.

Do not get carried away and serve too many varieties of smørrebrød. The sandwiches are very filling, and two make a meal for an average English appetite. If you want to have more varieties, cut the sandwiches into halves to make *snitters* or slices, and if you really want to show off, make cocktail-size smørrebrød in as many varieties as you wish.

Assembled sandwiches should be divided into categories and kept together so that they will not pick up the flavour of other sandwich toppings. Keep all the fish smørrebrød together, all the meat together, etc., both as you make them and as you serve them. No sandwich should ever touch another.

The sandwiches can be stored for a short time in the refrigerator or in a cool larder. Place them on baking sheets or trays lined with waxed paper, and cover them with clean kitchen towels that have been dampened and wrung dry. Add garnishes at the last moment so that they do not lose their freshness and crispness.

Though the smørrebrød should look neat, it is absolutely permissible for the meat or other topping to hang over the edges of the bread, since all big Danish open-faced sandwiches are eaten with a fork and knife. To hold cocktail-size ones together, fasten a toothpick through all the toppings. The end of the toothpick will help people lift the appetizer off the tray.

Bread

The bread *must* be firm and closely grained, so that it will not pull apart or tear in buttering. The bread should also be thinly sliced, which is possible with close-textured bread. Most smørrebrød is made with different kinds of rye bread, ranging from very dark to blond, and including the well-known Scandinavian crisp breads. Whole wheat bread is also good. White bread, which in Denmark is called *franskbrød* or French bread, must be of the firm, home-style kind.

The bread used should complement the flavour and texture of the topping, which in Danish is called *pålaeg*. A good general rule, allowing exceptions for personal taste, is that a soft bread is best with a firm topping, such as smoked ham, salami, etc., while a hard bread asks for a soft topping, such as liverwurst, fish, salads, etc. White bread is generally used for prawn and smoked salmon sandwiches, and for cheese. The very dark bread we know as pumpernickel also makes a good base for cheese.

Butter and Other Spreads

Danish butter, widely sold in England, is superb. The role of the butter in smørrebrød is not only to blend with the flavours of the topping but to prevent the topping from making the bread soggy. (Lettuce also does this.) The butter should be spread to the edges of the bread. How thickly depends on whether you are a Dane or an Englishman; for our tastes, the Danes spread their butter far too thickly.

Though the word '*smørre*' means buttering, it also means 'to spread', and other spreads besides butter are used for the sandwiches in Denmark. Spiced lard, pork dripping, duck and goose fat, lightly salted, are favourite Danish spreads. One of the most popular sandwiches consists of a piece of rye bread spread with pork dripping and a little coarse salt. But whatever the spread used, it should complement the flavour of the topping.

Garnishes

Chives, *Dill*, and *Parsley*. These are essentials. If no chives are at hand, use the finely chopped green tops of spring onions.

Rings. An onion cut into rings may be used instead of chopped onion because it looks more decorative. But often an onion ring is used to encircle a raw egg yolk, to prevent it from slipping off the sandwich. If an onion ring is unsuitable for the taste of the topping, as in the case of salmon, tomato rings are used instead. The tomato is sliced and the centre cut out.

Spriglets and *Snippets*. A spriglet is the smallest head of parsley, dill, or watercress. A snippet is a tiny piece of firm tomato, with some of the skin on, used mainly to give colour.

Springer. A slice of tomato, lemon, cucumber, or beetroot used as a garnish. A cut is made in the slice, from one side through the centre and halfway to the opposite side. By twisting in opposite directions, the slices can be made to stand up on the smørrebrød. Cucumber and lemon springer are often dusted with paprika.

Strips. Smørrebrød arrangements in strips or stripes are common. Minced onion, scrambled egg, caviar, chopped egg, spinach, salads, etc., are often put crosswise or in parallel strips on a sandwich.

Eggs. Raw eggs are part of some sandwiches, such as a beef tartare or a Blue cheese smørrebrød. Only the yolk is used, and it is mashed up with the other ingredients before eating.

Hard-boiled egg slices, of course, are a very common ingredient or decoration.

New to English people is the use of scrambled eggs on sandwiches, especially with salmon, a classical combination, or with ham or herring. Danish scrambled eggs are not what we mean by them, but an unsweetened baked custard (*æggestand*) cut cold into ¾-inch-long strips, which are about 1 inch wide and ½ inch thick. However, Danish scrambled eggs are fairly tasteless, and English scrambled eggs, though not so lissomely elegant, have a far better flavour.

How to Make Smørrebrød

Unless a book is devoted to nothing else, it is impossible to list the hundreds and hundreds of smørrebrød combinations. I must therefore limit myself to a few words on the actual arrangement of the toppings.

Lettuce will set off any food to advantage. Even if you don't want to line the bread of the sandwich with it, use a little at either end, peering out from under the topping.

When a sandwich recipe calls for *mustard*, it is a good idea to sprinkle a little dry mustard powder or to spread prepared mustard thinly and directly on the butter, *under* the topping.

Egg slices should be arranged overlapping slightly.

Meat slices also should overlap. Ham looks attractive when rolled, and so does salami. The same applies to salmon.

Asparagus, even one tip only, is a valuable decorative asset. Insert it in a ham or salmon roll, so that the tip is visible. Or contain two or three short asparagus stalks in a ring of red pimento or green pepper, and lay them on the meat or other toppings.

Pickles are far better-looking when cut into strips and placed diagonally on a sandwich.

Grated horse-radish, chopped pickles, onions, eggs (chop the whites and the yolks of the hard-boiled eggs separately), and *caviar* can be arranged in tiny mounds (about ¼ teaspoon) or in strips around, across, or parallel with the topping.

Mushroom caps, sautéed in a little butter but still firm and light, are an excellent sandwich garnish, especially when they are fluted.

A *salad*, such as a herring or Italian salad, is best placed within a raw onion ring to contain it on the sandwich.

One *caper* looks untidy, but three or four, preferably topped with a parsley spriglet, look delightful on an egg and tomato smørrebrød.

Gelée, clear meat aspic, much used on smørrebrød, may be cut either into strips or into small, neat cubes, or coarsely chopped.

Ham, salami, meat, or salmon *cornucopias*, filled with a suitable salad or scrambled eggs, are attractive. Place a parsley spriglet on the filling.

Alternate slices of meat, eggs, tomatoes, or alternative strips of topping look appetizing when chosen with an eye to colour, as well as taste, especially when they are placed diagonally across a piece of smørrebrød. They may be topped at right angles with strips of meat, etc.

Radish roses are decorative and colourful.

Mayonnaise, plain or fancy, looks best when piped through a pastry tube, in strips, swirls, rosettes, etc.

Caviar, naturally, glorifies any smørrebrød or koldt bord. The Danish variety comes from lumpfish, and it is black and small-grained, and surprisingly good. Danish caviar can be bought in this country, and it is extremely worth while to have a jar at hand.

Standard Smørrebrød

Egg and Tomato. Place overlapping slices of hard-boiled egg on one half of buttered rye, crisp, or whole-wheat bread, and overlapping slices of firm tomatoes on the other half. Garnish with water cress.

Egg and Anchovy. Place overlapping slices of hard-boiled egg in two or more rows on buttered rye, crisp, brown, or whole-wheat bread. Place 2 or 3 thin fillets of anchovies diagonally across the egg slices. Garnish with radish slices or rosettes.

Egg with Tomato and Horse-radish. As above, but substitute strips of fresh or prepared horse-radish for the anchovy and garnish with tomato snippets.

Egg with Anchovy and Capers. Place anchovy fillets in parallel rows on buttered rye, crisp, brown, or whole-wheat bread. Chop hard-boiled egg and arrange it between the rows of anchovies. Garnish with capers.

Egg and Pickles. Arrange rows of overlapping slices of hard-boiled egg on buttered rye, crisp, brown, or whole-wheat bread. Garnish with little mounds of chopped sweet or dill pickles.

Egg with Curry Mayonnaise and Anchovy. Place slices of hard-boiled egg on rye or crisp bread. Pipe mayonnaise mixed with curry powder over egg slices in strips. Decorate with anchovy snippets. Or use remoulade sauce, omitting the anchovy.

Chopped Egg and Herring. Combine chopped egg and any kind of smoked, pickled, or salted chopped herring. Spread on buttered rye, crisp, or brown bread. Top with watercress or parsley spriglets. Or place chopped, boned herrings or herring strips lengthwise on chopped or overlapping slices of hard-boiled egg.

Smoked Herrings and Egg Yolks. Place strips of smoked herring fillets on buttered rye or brown bread. Leave some space in the middle for an onion ring. Place a raw egg yolk in the onion ring and pile raw onions or chopped radishes at both sides of the yolk.

NOTE: *Slide the raw egg yolk on this and on all raw egg yolk sandwiches from a spoon.*

Anchovies with Fried or Scrambled Egg and Chives. Place Danish- or English-style scrambled egg on buttered rye or whole wheat bread. Or use a freshly fried egg, sunny side up. Garnish with anchovy fillets placed crosswise on egg, and sprinkle with chives.

Sardine. Line a slice of buttered rye or whole-wheat bread with a small leaf of lettuce. Cover with small imported Danish sardines packed in tomato sauce. Sprinkle with chopped parsley and garnish with a twist of lemon.

Smoked Salmon and Scrambled Egg. Top buttered white bread with smoked salmon slices and, diagonally across the bread, a strip of cold scrambled egg. Decorate with chopped dill.

Lobster Salad. Combine chopped lobster, asparagus tips, and curry or tarragon mayonnaise. Line buttered rye or white bread with lettuce leaves and top with lobster salad. Garnish with additional lobster pieces and asparagus tips.

Roast Beef with Tomato and Cucumber. Place one or several slices cold roast beef on buttered rye, brown, or whole-wheat bread. Garnish with tomato slices and thinly sliced fresh or pickled cucumber.

Roast Beef with Remoulade Sauce. Top buttered bread with slices of cold roast beef and stripes of remoulade sauce.* Garnish with tomato snippets or twists.

Roast Beef with Horse-radish. Top buttered bread with slices of cold roast beef and garnish with grated or shaved fresh horse-radish. Top with French-fried onions.

Roast Beef with Potato Salad and Chives. Top slices of cold roast beef on buttered bread with a generous mound of well-seasoned potato salad bound with mayonnaise. Sprinkle with chopped chives.

Roast Beef and Ham with Cheese. Place a slice of ham on buttered dark bread and top with parallel strips of rare roast beef, as well as 3 strips of Camembert cheese placed at right angles on the beef. Sprinkle with paprika.

Brisket of Corned Beef and Horse-radish. Place meat slices on dark buttered bread. Sprinkle with grated or shaved fresh horse-radish and garnish with pickle strips and a tomato twist.

Steak and Fried Egg. Place strips of cold, juicy steak on buttered bread and top with hot fried egg. Serve immediately.

Roast Lamb and Cucumber Salad. Cover lamb slices or strips of meat on buttered bread with drained pickled cucumbers. Garnish with dill, parsley, or tomato.

Roast Pork and Beetroot. Place slices of cold roast pork on buttered dark bread and garnish with a twist of beetroot and a little jellied non-fat gravy. Or simply use onion rings or chopped onion and chopped pickles.

Tongue and Horse-radish. Place slices of cold tongue on dark bread buttered with mustard butter,* or on plainly buttered bread. Sprinkle with grated horse-radish in either case.

Bacon, Onion, and Apples. Place slices of crisp bacon on *unbuttered* dark bread. Top with crisp fried onion rings and a slice of fried apple.

Bacon and Mushrooms. Top dark buttered bread with crisp fried bacon slices and sliced fried mushrooms or creamed mushrooms.

Hard-boiled Eggs and Russian Herring Salad or Italian Salad.** Top dark buttered bread with overlapping slices of hard-boiled egg and generous helpings of one or the other salad.

Liver Pâté with Beetroot. Spread dark bread with butter or spiced pork fat* and top with slices of Mrs Jensen's liver pâté.* Garnish with chopped meat aspic* or a strip of beetroot or a pickle slice.

Frikadeller (Danish Meat Balls) with Cucumber Salad. Place sliced *frikadeller* (meat balls)* on buttered bread. Garnish with cucumber salad. Or top meat ball slices with aspic* strips and shredded red cabbage.

Smoked Eel. A Danish speciality. Place strips of smoked eel fillet on buttered rye bread and place a little scrambled egg between fish strips.

Roast Chicken. Spread dark or light rye with butter and sprinkle with a little grated fresh horse-radish. Top with thin slices of roast chicken. Garnish with liver pâté* pushed through a pastry tube and with sliced cucumber.

Chicken Salad. Line a slice of buttered white bread with a lettuce leaf. Top with chicken salad. Garnish with a tiny triangle of pineapple placed in the middle of the chicken salad and green or blue grapes leading from the pineapple to the four corners of the bread.

Camembert. Spread buttered brown bread with Camembert cheese and top with overlapping radish slices.

Cucumber Blue Cheese. Cut both ends off a small cucumber. Core, taking care not to break the shell. Stuff with an equal mixture of Blue cheese and cream or cottage cheese that have been blended together. Chill and cut cucumber into thin slices. Place cucumber slices on buttered dark or white bread. Top with coarsely chopped salted nuts.

Ham and Chicken. Spread toasted white bread with mustard butter.* Top one half of the bread with minced ham and the other with minced chicken bound with a little double cream or mayonnaise. Decorate with watercress.

Ham and Egg. Mash hard-boiled egg yolks with a little

prepared mustard and add a little finely chopped lettuce. Spread on buttered white bread and top with ham cut in strips. Sprinkle with a little grated orange peel.

Festive Smørrebrød

Shrimp (*Rejer*). This is the king of all smørrebrød, a universal favourite eaten in enormous numbers during the fresh-shrimp season. Made with the infinitesimal Danish shrimps, the flavour is good beyond words, but a very acceptable substitute can be made with the canned shrimps imported from Denmark. A minimum of 25 shrimps are placed on buttered white bread, shoulders and tail resting on the butter. A better sandwich is made from 50 to 60, or more, layered or arranged in a pyramid. Serve with lemon twists and freshly ground black pepper.

Beef Tartare. A slice of dark or light rye bread is buttered and covered with a large spoonful of freshly ground (or, better still, freshly scraped) sirloin or tenderloin *which must be raw*. Make a well in the centre of the beef and place an onion ring on it. Slip an egg yolk into the onion ring. Garnish with mounds or strips of grated fresh horse-radish, grated onion, anchovy fillets, and capers.

Smoked Salmon with Spinach and Mushroom Caps. Place overlapping slices of smoked salmon on dark buttered bread. Top grilled mushroom caps on spinach. Or substitute asparagus tips for spinach.

Ham and Chicken Salad. Place cornucopias of ham filled with chicken salad on buttered white bread. Garnish with parsley or dill sprigs.

Goose Liver Pâté with Ham and Madeira. Place thinly sliced ham on buttered dark or white bread. Top with spoonfuls of goose liver pâté. Sprinkle with chopped madeira aspic and garnish with watercress. Madeira aspic is a clear meat aspic* to which a little madeira has been added for flavouring.

Danish Blue Cheese and Egg. Spread Danish Blue cheese on buttered white bread, making a well in the centre of the cheese. Place an egg yolk in the well. Decorate with radish roses or slices. When eating the sandwich, break the egg yolk and spread it evenly across the cheese.

Fried Fish Fillets with Remoulade Sauce. In Denmark plaice is used for this sandwich, but it can be done with sole or other filleted white fish. Season a 4-inch-square piece of fish fillet with salt and pepper. Dip into 2 dessertspoons milk, then into 2 dessertspoons dry bread crumbs. Melt 2 dessertspoons butter and fry fish in it on both sides. Place warm fish on buttered or unbuttered white bread, and top with 2 dessertspoons remoulade sauce.* Or place fish on plate and serve bread separately.

Hans Christian Andersen's Sandwich. (I won't swear to the authenticity but I will swear to the taste.) Butter 1 slice white bread with ½ oz. butter. Place 2 slices crisply fried bacon on top. Top with 4 paper-thin slices of firm tomato and 2 thin slices of Mrs Jensen's liver pâté.* Garnish with 2 or 3 cubes meat aspic* and 1 teaspoon grated fresh horse-radish.

Liver Pâté and Tongue. Butter 1 slice white or dark bread with 1 tablespoon butter. Place 2 finger-length slices of liver pâté* on 2 slices of tongue or boiled ham and roll. Top bread with meat rolls and garnish with sliced or chopped sweet or dill pickles and parsley sprigs.

The Vet's Midnight Supper. Spread 1 slice dark or light rye bread with 2 dessertspoons pork dripping or meat jelly. Top with 2 slices of liver pâté,* chopped meat aspic,* and thin slices of cold spiced breast of veal.* Decorate with watercress.

Lobster. Blend about ½ cup cold chopped lobster with 2 dessertspoons double cream and season with salt and pepper to taste. Spread 1 slice of white bread with ½ oz. butter. Top with lobster. Place about 2 dessertspoons cold chopped lobster in a cup made with a lettuce leaf and set this on creamed lobster. Serve with lemon twists.

Marrow. Boil 2 2-inch pieces of marrow bone for about 5 to 10 minutes. Remove marrow from bone and spread on 1 slice of dry rye toast. Sprinkle with coarse salt.

Scrambled Egg with Mussels and Spinach. Beat 1 egg with 2 teaspoons water and 1 dessertspoon melted butter. Cook over low heat, stirring until scrambled. Place 6 mussels (well scrubbed) in a pan. Shake over low heat until mussels open.

Remove mussels from shells. Steam ½ cup fresh, finely chopped spinach until tender, about 2 to 3 minutes. Drain thoroughly. Spread 2 slices of bread with 1 oz. butter. Place strips of scrambled egg, spinach, and rows of mussels diagonally across the bread. Makes 2 sandwiches.

Meat Salad. Combine ¼ cup finely chopped cold beef, veal, or pork with 2 dessertspoons plain or flavoured mayonnaise. Spread on buttered dark bread and sprinkle with chopped onion, diced cucumbers, or pickles.

Cod or Shad Roe Salad. Cover roe with boiling salted water. Simmer over low heat for 30 to 40 minutes or until firm. Remove skin. Press roe through a sieve. Season with salt and pepper to taste. Stir in 1 dessertspoon lemon juice and ½ teaspoon curry powder. Spread on slices of dark or white bread which have been buttered with ½ oz. butter each. Garnish with watercress and lemon twists. This will serve 2 or 3 depending on size of roe.

Meats, Salads, and other Smørrebrød Toppings and Koldt Bord Dishes

Generally speaking, these are the dishes found on a good smørgasbord. The sky's the limit, provided the combinations are judiciously matched to each other, as to both flavour and texture. When you put these spreads on the smørrebrød, remember that the bread used should complement the toppings.

DUCK OR GOOSE DRIPPING

The flavour of both of these is excellent, but both have a tendency to be too liquid to be spread on bread. To remedy this, blend a little melted lard into the dripping – just enough to achieve proper spreading consistency. Chill before using.

SPICED PORK FAT

This is used on certain smørrebrød, especially those topped with smoked meats, liver pâté, and salami or other sausages.

The easiest kind is made by melting pure lard or fat pork. Fry a little minced onion and a little thyme, or crushed sage, or a tiny amount of crushed bay leaf in the hot fat, but do not brown the onion. Strain and chill before using. The quantity of these ingredients depends on personal taste.

FLAVOURED BUTTERS AND MAYONNAISE

Use these for spreading on smørrebrød. If stored in a covered container in the refrigerator, they will keep for a week or so.

Lemon Butter. Cream ¼ lb. softened butter. Gradually stir in 2 dessertspoons lemon juice and, if desired, 2 dessertspoons finely chopped parsley or dill.

Curry Butter. Cream ¼ lb. softened butter. Stir in ½ teaspoon curry powder and a little black pepper or a dash of hot pepper sauce.

Mustard Butter. Cream ¼ lb. softened butter. Stir in 1 teaspoon or more prepared mustard, or ¼ to ½ teaspoon dry mustard.

Anchovy Butter. Cream ¼ lb. softened butter. Stir in anchovy paste to taste, starting with ¼ teaspoon.

Tomato Mayonnaise. Add 2 teaspoons tomato purée to 1 cup mayonnaise.

Mustard Mayonnaise. Add 2 teaspoons prepared mustard to 1 cup mayonnaise.

Cucumber Mayonnaise. Add ½ cup finely chopped cucumber and 1 teaspoon chopped parsley to 1 cup mayonnaise. Good for fish sandwiches.

Horse-radish Mayonnaise. Add a little grated fresh or prepared horse-radish to taste to mayonnaise.

NOTE: *Both butters and mayonnaise may be flavoured in any desired way, to suit personal tastes – and the topping that will be used in the sandwich. Instant onion and garlic, powdered herbs, bottled sauces, and spices all lend themselves as flavourings.*

Danish Blue Cheese Spread

6 oz. Danish Blue cheese
6 oz. unsalted butter, softened
2 teaspoons grated onion
Dash Tabasco
1 cup finely chopped blanched salted almonds

Mash Danish Blue cheese with a fork until smooth. Beat in butter, grated onion, and Tabasco. Blend thoroughly. Form into a ball and roll in chopped almonds. Chill before serving. Or make individual servings by shaping cheese mixture into tiny balls and rolling in chopped almonds.

Herring Salad 1 · *Sildesalat*

Herring salad is a favourite throughout Scandinavia, and though the basic ingredients remain the same, each cook uses the quantities of each she prefers. Personally, I like a salad that does not taste too powerfully of herring.

Danish cooks make a 'fine' herring salad by omitting the cream or white sauce dressing, chopping all the ingredients on a chopping board until they form a soft mixture. This is good for spreading on smørrebrød, but a diced salad (as below) with some body to it tastes better, to my mind.

1 salt herring, filleted, or 1 5 oz. jar Bismarck herring, or more
1 cup diced cold boiled potatoes
1 cup diced pickled beets
½ cup diced peeled apples
⅓ cup diced onion
1 teaspoon mustard
1 teaspoon sugar
1 dessertspoon vinegar
8 fl. oz. thick white sauce, cold, or ⅔ cup double cream, whipped
Salt
Pepper

Soak herring overnight in cold water. Drain and dice. Combine all ingredients except white sauce or cream, salt, and pepper. Blend with white sauce or whipped cream, and season with salt and pepper to taste. Chill before using.

NOTE: *The dressing should barely hold the salad together.*

Herring Salad 2 · *Sildesalat*

Add 1 cup cooked chopped meat to above ingredients. Increase seasonings, if desired, adding ¼ cup chopped mixed pickles. If necessary, use more white sauce or whipped cream to bind the salad. Decorate with chopped parsley and slices of hard-boiled eggs.

Italian Salad · *Italiensk Salat*

1 cup diced cooked carrots
1 cup cooked asparagus, finely cut
1 cup cooked small green peas
Mayonnaise
Tarragon vinegar or lemon juice
Dry mustard

Combine carrots, asparagus, and peas. Thin mayonnaise with a little tarragon vinegar or lemon juice and stir in a little dry mustard. Toss vegetables in mayonnaise and chill. If this salad is to be used on smørrebrød, be sure to place a lettuce leaf on the buttered bread before topping it with the salad. The lettuce will prevent the bread from becoming soggy.

Variation: Add either or both ½ cup cooked elbow or shell macaroni and 1 cup ham or tongue cut into julienne strips.

Chicken Salad · *Hønsesalat*

2 cups diced white chicken meat
1 cup celeriac cut in julienne strips or chopped celery
8 fl. oz. double cream
½ teaspoon mild mustard or more, to taste
Salt
Pepper
Lettuce
Capers
Tomato twists

Combine chicken and celeriac. Whip cream until slightly stiffened. Stir in mustard and salt and pepper to taste. Fold chicken mixture into cream. Pile on lettuce leaves and decorate with capers and tomato twists.

Spiced Breast of Veal · *Rullepølse*

This recipe, the best I know for the dish, comes from Mr Craig Claiborne, the distinguished food editor of the *New York Times*, who is an accomplished chef. The sliced meat may be used for smørrebrød, but it is also delicious for a cold buffet.

1 breast of veal
1 lb. salt pork, sliced
1 dessertspoon freshly ground black pepper
2 dessertspoons salt
1 dessertspoon saltpetre
1 dessertspoon ground allspice
1 cup chopped onions
5 dessertspoons finely chopped dill or parsley
Brine

Have the butcher bone the breast of veal and flatten it. Trim it to make a large square. Arrange the salt pork on the veal and sprinkle with pepper, salt, saltpetre, allspice, onions, and dill or parsley. Roll the veal jelly-roll fashion, wrap the meat roll in a clean white cloth, tie tightly with string, and place in a brine bath prepared according to directions below. Weigh it down with a heavy plate or other weight and let it rest in a cool place for 5 or 6 days. Drain the veal. Place it in a large pan and cover with water. Add salt to taste and bring to the boil. Simmer, covered, 1½ hours. Remove from cooking liquid and weigh down once more. Refrigerate at least 24 hours. Remove the cloth. Cut into wafer-thin slices. To prepare brine bath, place enough cold water in a crock to cover the rolled veal. Dissolve enough salt in the water so that a medium-sized potato will float in the brine. Stir in ¼ teaspoon saltpetre.

Pickled Herring · *Syltesild*

Few Danish housewives pickle their own herring nowadays, since there are scores of different preserved herring on the market, all excellent. Many wonderful pickled, spiced, and other herring are imported into England from Denmark, as well as other Scandinavian countries, and I would advise my readers to do as the Danes. But for those with an urge to pickle their own, here goes:

10 herring
4 onions, sliced
⅗ pint white vinegar
⅖ pint water
⅔ cup sugar
4 teaspoons whole allspice
3 bay leaves
12 black peppercorns

Clean fish, cut off heads, and soak overnight in cold water. Drain. Remove bones and skin and cut in halves lengthwise. Cut crosswise into ½-inch slices. Place slices in bowl, in alternate layers with onions. Combine all other ingredients and bring to the boil. Cool. Pour mixture over herring and onions. Cover and store in refrigerator for at least 12 hours or longer. Drain before using, and use only the herring.

NOTE: *According to taste, the amount of vinegar may be increased and the sugar decreased. Mustard and horse-radish may be added to the pickling liquid. In short, there are dozens of ways of flavouring the pickled herring.*

Mrs Jensen's Liver Pâté · *Leverpostej*

Liver pâté is a regular part of the Danish diet, and there are as many recipes for it as there are Danish cooks. Generally the pâté is not like the densely textured French pâté, but more along the lines of a very firm soufflé. Mrs Jensen is the lady who first introduced me to the delights of Danish home cooking.

2 lb. pork or calf's liver
1 medium-sized onion
1 lb. pork fat
2 oz. butter
4 dessertspoons flour
⅘ pint single cream
2 eggs, well beaten
2 teaspoons anchovy paste (or less, or more, according to taste)
2 teaspoons salt
1 teaspoon pepper
½ teaspoon ground ginger

With the finest blade of the mincer, mince liver and onion twice. Mince pork fat twice. Melt butter and stir in flour. Gradually stir in cream, and cook over low heat, stirring constantly, until thickened and smooth. Add minced pork fat and stir until fat has melted. Remove from heat. Add liver and all other ingredients and blend thoroughly. Spoon into 2-quart baking-dish. Place dish in baking pan with hot water. Bake in 325° F., gas mark 3, oven for 1½ to 2 hours, or until pâté tests clean. Cover with lid or aluminium foil if top is browning too quickly. Replenish water in baking pan if necessary. Cool before serving on smørrebrød or the cold table.

Warm Smørrebrød · *Varmt Smørrebrød*

Warm appetizers are occasionally served in Denmark, as well as a 'little warm dish' (*småretter*) to follow the cold smørrebrød. The appetizers are not basically different from ours, consisting of little filled cheese puffs,* bacon or sausage morsels, and puff-paste patties and tartlets made with a rich dough and filled with a deliciously rich filling.* Danish hot appetizers are beautiful, because, like the open-faced sandwiches, each is composed to look like a colourful picture.

The 'little warm dish' may be any warm dish that is not elaborate. Minced meat dishes, with boiled potatoes, would be the choice of most Danes, but there is no reason that a simple fish dish would not serve.

The recipes for warm appetizers that follow are to be looked upon as samples rather than a total listing. I refer my readers to their standard cookbooks, and books for cocktail and party entertaining, where they'll find any number of suitable recipes.

Lobster or Prawn Patties · *Hummer eller reje postej*

1 oz. butter
1½ dessertspoons flour
8 fl. oz. milk
2½ fl. oz. double cream
2 egg yolks, well beaten
2 dessertspoons cognac
½ teaspoon dry mustard
Salt
Cayenne
1 cup diced boiled lobster meat, or 1 cup chopped cooked shelled prawns
½ lb. mushrooms, sliced
1 oz. butter
Patty shells, heated

Melt butter in top of double boiler over very low heat. Stir in flour and cook over very low heat about 3 minutes, stirring constantly. Gradually stir in milk and cook over very low heat until smooth and thickened, stirring all the time. Place top of double boiler over lower portion, filled with simmering water. Cook sauce about 15 minutes, stirring occasionally (practically all white sauces are undercooked, and taste raw). Remove sauce from bottom of double boiler and place over direct heat. Cook it down to three fourths of its volume, stirring constantly. Remove from heat and stir in cream. Beat together egg yolks, cognac, and dry mustard. Beat mixture into hot sauce, a little at a time. Season with salt and and a little cayenne to taste. Add lobster or prawns to sauce and cook for about 3 minutes over boiling water. Cook mushrooms in hot butter until softened but still firm and white. Add to lobster or prawn mixture. Spoon into patty shells and serve immediately.

NOTE: *The mixture may also be served in tartlet shells. If these are very small, omit sautéed mushrooms, but garnish with a sliver of raw mushroom sprinkled with a little lemon juice to keep it white.*

Variation: To make a very Danish looking dish, prepare a rich pie crust dough sufficient for a 9-inch single crust. Make up the above lobster or prawn recipe in double or triple quantities and place in shallow baking-dish. Roll out dough in strips and make a lattice the size of the baking-dish. Place lattice on filling and bake at 425° F., gas mark 7, until golden brown. Place additional sea food in lattice cavities.

Filled Cheese Puffs · *Vandbakkelsedejg med Fyld*

8 fl. oz. water
2 oz. butter
1 cup sifted flour
3 eggs, at room temperature
1 oz. grated Parmesan or other cheese
½ teaspoon salt
⅛ teaspoon pepper

Combine water and butter and bring to the boil. Remove from heat. Add flour all at once. Beat until glossy over a low flame, until dough does not cling to the sides of the pan any longer. Remove from heat; do not overcook, or puffs won't rise in baking. Beat in eggs, one at a time. Beat in cheese, salt, and pepper. Shape with pastry bag or spoon on ungreased baking-sheet. Place puffs about 2 inches apart to allow spreading. Bake in preheated 400° F., gas mark 6, oven for 10 minutes. Reduce heat to 350° F., gas mark 4, and bake 20 to 25 minutes longer. Do not remove puffs from oven until quite firm to the touch. Prick with a fork at the side of the puffs. Replace in oven for 5 minutes to allow puffs to dry. Cool away from draughts before filling. For filling, cut puffs horizontally with a sharp knife. Fill with creamed eggs, chicken, sea food, ham, or a heavy cheese sauce. Makes about 12 medium-sized puffs.

Ham Filling for Tartlets

½ cup finely chopped shallots
1 oz. butter
2 cups shredded Danish ham or canned loin of pork or gammon
5 fl. oz. sour cream
2 egg yolks
¼ cup finely chopped parsley or dill
Dash Tabasco

Cook shallots in hot butter until soft and golden. Add meat and cook over low heat about 5 minutes, or until thoroughly heated through. Stir constantly. Beat sour cream with egg yolks, parsley, or dill, and Tabasco. Add to meat mixture and cook until just heated. Do not boil. Use as a filling for tiny tartlets, patties, cheese puffs, or spread on hot toast.

Danish Cheese

Denmark makes, eats, and exports some of the best cheeses in the world. Many of these can be bought in England, and I strongly advise my readers to get to know them, to their lasting benefit.

The Danes use their cheese for eating rather than for cooking. Cheese is the inevitable end of a smørrebrød lunch, and cheese is greatly appreciated for dessert. In this case it is served with fruit, especially with grapes, an excellent combination and an interesting variation from the more familiar cheese and apple or pear combinations.

The best known of all Danish cheeses is the Blue cheese and a mighty fine Blue cheese it is too. Danish Blue has a cousin by the name of Mycella, which is far richer and creamier, and about one of the world's best blue-veined cheeses. Most Danish cheeses are on the smooth, golden, and mild side. There is the Samsø, which resembles a baby Swiss and has a firm texture, a mild flavour, and tiny holes; Tybo, an Edam-type cheese; Havarti, which reminds one of Tilsit; and Esrom, along the lines of a Port Salut. (These comparisons do not mean that Danish cheese does not have a character of its own; they are made for the benefit of readers who might not be familiar with Danish cheeses.)

The granddaddy of all the Danish cheeses is Samsø, with its various offspring such as Danbo, Fynbo, and Elbo. There are also many other speciality cheeses of a very superior quality, such as Christian IX, which contains caraway seeds, and an absolutely heavenly cream cheese, Crema Danica.

The quality of Danish cheese is uniformly excellent, thanks to the guidance and supervision of the Federation of Danish Dairy Associations. I've seen quite a number of dairies, and I can only report that their cleanliness is that of a surgery and their equipment of the most modern. The control begins with the milk; the cheese-master knows the specific qualities of each can that comes to the dairy so that he can allot it for making the cheese it is best suited for. As for the Danish cows, they must be the world's healthiest and best looked after. All the herds are registered, the stock is constantly improved, and from birth to death they get the care reserved in many countries only for the children of the rich. I've often wished to be reincarnated as a Danish cow; I can't think of a more pleasant life.

There is a form of entertaining in Denmark that greatly took my fancy because it is suited to English life. That is the cheese party, and a good time for one is after the theatre or as an evening entertainment. The most elegant cheese party I went to was given by Didder Pedersen, the petite and chic wife of the then manager of Pan American's Copenhagen office, a man with the disposition of a saint. Didder is an energetic woman, and besides being a wife, mother, and large-scale entertainer, she is also one of the best-known Danish women journalists. She had set the table with her magnificent antique silver, and displayed the food as if it were a picture. Here are the highlights: Danish Blue cheese mixed in equal parts with unsweetened whipped cream, stiffened with a little gelatin, and moulded into a ring filled with marinated asparagus. Danish Camembert, crumbed and deep fried, kept warm in a chafing dish and utterly delicious. A salad of Samsø cheese resting on blades of Belgian endives. A Gypsy cheese salad surrounded by little mounds of marinated mixed vegetables and salami cornucopias. Danish cream cheese, far creamier than ours, whipped frothy with a little cream and mixed with finely chopped blanched almonds, raisins, and candied fruits, presented on pale green lettuce leaves. There was also a large silver tray with a score or more cheese appetizers, and a noble hunk of Havarti, surrounded by perfect, enormous blue grapes and pineapple sticks. A glorious piece of Mycella came with apples and pears, and I think this is the best dessert of them all. A large tossed salad kept company with the cheeses, and so did a large platter of assorted dark and light breads and crocks of Denmark's irresistible butter. For drinks, we had a choice of beer or Bordeaux. I've never forgotten Didder's cheese party.

Soups and Dumplings

Soups and Dumplings

A good Danish soup is a substantial dish, and some of them make the whole meal, followed by a little dessert or a bite of cheese, perhaps. Other soups are silky and smooth, because the Danes don't believe that you can make good soup from odds and ends and a drop of broth or water.

Fruit and sweet soups are very popular in Denmark, as in all of Scandinavia. Sometimes they are eaten at the beginning of a meal, sometimes at the end. When a foreigner can be induced to eat such soups on their own merit, he will like them. I often serve them as refreshing desserts, and to children, who love them.

Cereal gruels and porridges used to be part of Denmark's

national diet. Today they are fast becoming obsolete, thanks to modern foods and modern methods of food preservation. In the old days these cereal gruels and porridges were the main standby of the country people and the lower-income groups. Now Danish eating is lighter and more varied, although on the farms, and also in the towns, these dishes are still eaten as fillers before the fish or meat dish. And Danish children eat them far oftener than our children eat porridge, since they take the place of cold cereals.

Macaroni, spaghetti, and noodles are not part of the Danish national diet; barley, groats, and similar grains take their place. Nor is rice part of Denmark's food inheritance, with the exception of *risengrød*, a rice porridge which is still part of the traditional Danish Christmas dinner. The recipe for this dish will be found in the dessert chapter.

Some of the traditional soups in this chapter are not often found in restaurants, and this is a pity. Sometimes they can be prepared to order, and this is well worth while.

The recipes in this chapter may easily be doubled and even tripled.

Cauliflower Soup · *Blomkaalssuppe*

1 medium-sized cauliflower
2 oz. butter
2 dessertspoons grated onion
2 dessertspoons grated celery
2 dessertspoons flour
32 fl. oz. hot chicken bouillon
16 fl. oz. hot milk or single cream
Salt
White pepper
1 or 2 egg yolks
2 fl. oz. double cream
2 dessertspoons madeira

Trim cauliflower. Cook in rapidly boiling water. Drain; divide into flowerets. Reserve about one fourth of the flowerets. Force remaining cauliflower through a strainer or a food mill or purée in blender. Melt butter and cook onion and celery in it for 2 minutes. Stir in flour. Do not brown. Gradually stir in hot bouillon. Add strained cauliflower. Stir in hot milk or cream. Season with salt and pepper to taste. Cook over medium heat, stirring constantly, until sauce coats spoon. Beat egg yolks with cream. Remove soup from heat and gradually stir into egg yolks. Stir in madeira. Add cauliflowerets. Serve very hot, immediately.

Chervil Soup · *Koervelsuppe*

A spring and summer soup.

3 oz. butter
4 dessertspoons flour
2½ to 3 pints hot bouillon, depending on how thick a soup you want
Salt
Pepper
2 boiled carrots, sliced
⅓ cup minced fresh chervil
Poached eggs

Melt butter and stir in flour. Cook 2 minutes over medium heat, stirring constantly. Do not brown. Gradually stir in hot bouillon. Season with salt and pepper to taste. Simmer, covered, over low heat 15 minutes, stirring occasionally. Add sliced carrots and heat through. Just before serving, add chervil. Do not boil soup, or chervil will loose its delicate taste and fresh green colour. Serve with poached eggs; place 1 poached egg in each soup plate and ladle soup carefully over it.

Consommé with Port and Gilt

From Steensgaard, an enchanting sixteenth-century manor now run as a *pension* by its owner, the Countess Ella Bille Brahe Selby, who is an inspired cook. This soup is most elegant-looking.

2½ pints clear strong consommé
8 fl. oz. very good port
2 dessertspoons flaked gilt

Heat consommé and add port. Heat through thoroughly but do not boil. Serve in hot cups, with a sprinkle of gilt in each cup.

NOTE: *Gilt can be bought in artists' supply stores. It is inexpensive and totally harmless where consumed in the minute quantities called for by the recipe.*

Goose Giblet Soup · *Kraasesuppe*

The Danes are very fond of goose and of thick, nourishing soups. Since they are also very thrifty, the aftermath of a goose is this soup, a meal in itself.

Gizzard, neck, wings, feet, and heart of a goose
1½ pints water
4 carrots, peeled and sliced
½ cup sliced celery
4 leeks, sliced
4 whole peppercorns
2 teaspoons salt
6 medium-sized tart apples, peeled and cored
1 cup stoned prunes
2 oz. sugar
12 fl. oz. water
¼ lb. butter
2 oz. flour
2½ pints liquid from giblet stock and juices of apples and prunes
1 recipe dumplings*

Strip heavy membrane from gizzard. Cut neck into 3 pieces. Cut wings into 2 pieces. Clean feet, remove skin and claws. Wash heart. Place in a large pan and add water, vegetables, peppercorns, and salt. Bring to the boil. Simmer, covered, for 2 hours or until meat is tender. Strip meat from neck and wings. Cut meat, heart, and gizzard into small pieces. Replace meat in stock. Remove feet.

Peel and core apples. Cut into thin slices. Combine with prunes, sugar, and water. Cover, bring to the boil, and simmer until fruits are tender. Drain fruit; reserve fruit and liquid.

Combine meat, vegetables, stock, and juice drained from fruit and add enough water to make 2½ pints. Melt butter. Stir in flour. Gradually stir liquid mixture into butter and flour. Cook over low heat, stirring constantly, until smooth and thick. Add the apples and prunes. Make dumplings and place in hot soup.

NOTE: *If a thinner soup is wanted, add more hot water to make desired consistency.*

Meat Soup with Vegetables and Dumplings
Kødsuppe med Urter og Boller

The soup, with the vegetables, meat balls, and dumplings, is served as one course. The beef is sliced and served with boiled potatoes and horse-radish sauce.*

Soup

3 lb. beef shin with bone
About 2½ pints water
2 teaspoons salt
½ teaspoon pepper
½ cup diced celeriac or ½ cup sliced celery
½ cup diced carrots
½ cup sliced leeks or onions
1 dessertspoon chopped parsley

Meat Balls

¼ lb. lean raw pork
¼ lb. raw veal
1 dessertspoon flour
1 egg, well beaten
8 fl. oz. milk
½ teaspoon salt
¼ teaspoon pepper

Dumplings

3 oz. butter
2 oz. flour
4 fl. oz. boiling water
2 eggs, separated
½ teaspoon salt
¼ teaspoon sugar

To make *soup*, cover beef shin with water in a deep pan. Add salt and pepper. Bring to the boil, cover, and simmer 15 minutes. Remove scum with slotted spoon as it rises. Add vegetables. Cover and simmer 2 hours or until beef is tender. Remove beef and keep warm. Serve beef sliced as the main course with boiled potatoes and horse-radish sauce.*

To make *meat balls*, mince pork and veal together four times, using the finest blade of the mincer. Beat in flour, then beat in egg. Beat in milk, a small amount at a time. Beat in salt and pepper. Just before serving time, drop meat balls into boiling salted water. Simmer for 5 minutes in barely boiling water. Drain and add to hot soup at serving time.

To make *dumplings*, melt butter and stir in flour. Add boiling water. Over low heat, stir and beat until smooth. Chill mixture. Beat in egg yolks, salt, and sugar. Beat egg whites until stiff and fold in. Drop by teaspoonfuls into boiling salted water. Simmer until dumplings rise to the surface. Remove with a slotted spoon. Place dumplings in soup. Reheat soup slightly, without boiling, and serve.

Mushroom Soup with Madeira
Kalvesuppe med Madeira og Champignons

A delicious soup from the Hotel d'Angleterre in Copenhagen.

2½ fl. oz. water
⅛ teaspoon salt
½ dessertspoon lemon juice
½ oz. butter
¼ lb. very white mushrooms
1 oz. butter
2 dessertspoons flour
2½ to 3 pints hot white veal stock,* depending on how thick a soup you want
Salt
White pepper
2½ fl. oz. madeira or more, to taste

Bring water, salt, lemon juice, and butter to the boil in an enamel saucepan. (A metal saucepan will darken mushrooms, which must remain very white.) Trim and wash mushrooms; slice thinly. Add mushrooms to liquid and stir to cover them with the liquid. Simmer, covered, for 5 minutes, stirring or tossing frequently. In deep pan, melt 1 oz. butter and stir in flour. Gradually add hot stock, stirring constantly. Simmer, covered, for 10 minutes, stirring frequently. Season with salt and pepper to taste. Add mushrooms and mushroom liquid and heat through. Just before serving, remove from heat and stir in madeira.

NOTE: *For a richer soup, stir 3 to 4 fl. oz. double cream into soup before adding madeira.*

Yellow Pea Soup · *Gule Aerter*

Perhaps *the* national Danish soup and a meal in itself. The soup and the meats are served separately, with pickled beets, a good sharp mustard, dark rye bread and butter, and ice-cold *snaps* and beer. The Danes start with a plate of soup, and eat the second helping alternately with the meats and garnishes.

1½ cups yellow split peas
1½ pints water
1 teaspoon salt
1 lb. streaky bacon or salt pork in one piece
1 peeled and diced celeriac or 1 cup chopped celery
3 sliced leeks or 1 cup green onion tops
2½ pints water
3 sliced carrots
3 medium-sized potatoes, diced
1 large onion, chopped
1 lb. Danish gammon cut into ¼-inch slices
1 4-oz. can Danish or other tiny frankfurters, drained

Combine split peas, water, and salt. Bring to the boil and simmer until tender and very soft – about 1½ to 2 hours. Skim off pea skins as they float to the top. Force through a sieve or a food mill, or purée in blender. Place bacon or salt pork in a large saucepan. (If salt pork is very salty, soak in cold water for 30 minutes to 1 hour before using.) Add celery root and leeks or green onion tops. Add water. Cover and simmer for 1½ to 2 hours or until meat is tender. Add carrots, potatoes and onion. Cover and simmer until vegetables are tender. Remove bacon or salt pork. Cut into slices. Skim fat from broth or chill in refrigerator, remove fat, and reheat. Stir pea purée into broth. If necessary, add additional water until soup is the consistency of thick cream. Add sliced gammon and sausages cut into ½-inch pieces. Heat soup to the boiling point. Simmer 5 minutes. Remove gammon and serve slices with the slices of bacon or salt pork. Serve soup separately.

White Veal Stock

The base for many soups and sauces.

5 lb. veal bones, including knuckle, cracked
1 lb. veal, cut in pieces
4 chicken feet, cleaned and skinned
5 pints cold water
2 stalks celery, with tops, sliced
1 onion, sliced
1 carrot, sliced
3 sprigs parsley
2 teaspoons salt

Place veal bones, veal, and chicken feet in a deep pan and cover with water. Bring to the boil, and boil gently for 5 minutes. Drain and rinse bones, veal, and chicken feet under cold running water to remove all scum. (Veal produces a great deal of scum and this is the easiest way to remove it.) Rinse the pan free of all scum. Return bones, meat, and chicken feet to clean pan and cover with 5 pints water and remaining ingredients. Bring to the boil and simmer, covered, for 4 hours, skimming as necessary. Strain broth through a fine sieve lined with cheesecloth. Chill and remove fat. Store in refrigerator, where it will keep for 4 to 5 days. Makes about 2½ quarts white stock.

NOTE: *The liquid must really simmer as slowly as possible, with only a bubble or two on the surface.*

Chine of Pork Soup · *Svinerygsuppe*

A good one-dish meal that needs only rye bread and butter, a light dessert or some cheese or fruit.

4 lb. loin of pork
1 tablespoon salt
Water
1 medium-sized cabbage, shredded
1 celeriac, diced, or 1 cup sliced celery
2 carrots, sliced
4 peppercorns
Bouquet garni of 2 sprigs parsley, 2 sprigs dill, and 1 3-inch leek

Sprinkle pork with salt. Place meat in a large pan and cover with water. Bring to the boil. Skim with slotted spoon as scum rises. Cook for 15 minutes. Add cabbage, celery root, carrots, peppercorns, and bouquet garni. Simmer, covered, over lowest possible heat for 3 hours or until pork is tender. Remove bouquet garni and meat. Slice meat and serve on hot platter, with the hot soup.

Flour Dumplings · *Melboller*

Dumplings are part of traditional Danish cooking. They are served with meats as well as fruit soups, especially in the countryside, where the food is more substantial than in the towns.

2 oz. butter or margarine
2 oz. flour
4 fl. oz. water
2 eggs, separated
½ teaspoon salt
⅛ teaspoon cardamom

Melt butter. Stir in flour. Add water and stir batter over low heat until it leaves the sides of the pan. Remove from heat and cool. Beat in egg yolks, salt, and cardamom. Fold in stiffly beaten egg whites. With two teaspoons dipped in cold water, shape into tiny dumplings. Drop dumplings into boiling salted water. When the dumplings rise to the surface remove them with a slotted spoon. Place dumplings in tureen or individual soup plates and pour hot soup over them.

Apple Soup · *Aeblesuppe*

The soup should be the consistency of heavy cream.

1½ lb. tart apples
4 pints water
1 cinnamon stick
Rind of 1 lemon, cut into strips
1 oz. cornflour
4 fl. oz. water
2 oz. sugar
4 fl. oz. white wine
6 pieces zwieback or rusks
Whipped cream

Quarter and core apples. Do not peel. Place apples in a deep pan and add 1½ quarts of the water, cinnamon stick, and lemon rind. Cook over low heat until apples are very soft. Do not drain apples. Remove cinnamon stick. Force apples through a strainer or a food mill, or purée in blender. Add remaining quart of water. Blend cornflour in 4 fl. oz. water to a smooth paste. Stir into soup. Cook soup over low heat until thickened and smooth, stirring constantly. Add sugar and white wine. The soup should be tart but, if desired, add more sugar. Crush zwieback and distribute in 6 soup plates. Ladle soup over crumbs. Serve hot or cold with whipped cream.

Beer Soup · *Øllebrød*

This is a very old and very popular Danish dish; not a soup in our sense of the word, but a thick pottage. Unfortunately, it is seldom served to foreigners. The proper ingredients are a sweet dark non-alcoholic malt beer sometimes found in German and Scandinavian neighbourhoods and dark Danish rye bread. In lieu of the Danish *hvidtøl* a dark ale may be used and dark pumpernickel can be substituted for the bread. But the taste will not be the same.

8 slices pumpernickel
About 1 pint brown ale
8 fl. oz. water
Grated rind and juice of 1 lemon
Sugar
Plain or whipped cream

Break bread into small pieces. Place in deep dish. Combine ale and water and pour over bread. Soak at least 3 hours or overnight. Simmer over low heat until soup thickens to desired consistency. Force through strainer or purée in blender. Stir in lemon rind and juice. Sweeten to taste. Bring once more to the boil. Serve hot with plain or whipped cream.

Cold Buttermilk Soup · *Kaernemaelkskoldskål*

A surprisingly pleasant and refreshing dish for a hot-day supper. It is generally served with oat cakes.

2 eggs, well beaten
Juice and grated rind of 1 lemon
5 dessertspoons sugar
1 teaspoon vanilla
1½ pints buttermilk
8 fl. oz. double cream, whipped (optional)

Beat eggs with lemon juice, lemon rind, sugar, and vanilla. Whip buttermilk until frothy. Beat into egg mixture, a little at a time. Chill until frosty. Top with whipped cream. Serve with stewed fruit, preserves, or with oat cakes.*

Oat Cakes

¼ lb. butter
¼ lb. sugar
2 cups instant oatmeal

Melt butter and stir in sugar. Add oatmeal. Cook over medium heat until oatmeal is golden brown. Moisten egg cups, small individual baking-dishes, or tartlet tins with cold water and pack firmly with oatmeal mixture. Chill. Unmould and serve with buttermilk soup.

NOTE: *In Denmark the cakes are split and the soup poured over them.*

Hot Buttermilk Soup

Think of it as a dessert, rather than a soup in the Danish manner, and you'll like it after a heavy main dish.

¼ lb. rice
3¼ pints buttermilk
Grated rind of 1 lemon
1 stick cinnamon
⅓ cup raisins
2 egg yolks
1 dessertspoon sugar
Almonds
Whipped cream

Crush rice with meat pounder or hammer until the consistency of coarse salt. (This is best done by placing the rice in a heavy paper bag or wrapping it in a kitchen towel.) Combine rice and buttermilk. Add lemon rind, cinnamon, and raisins. Cook over low heat, stirring constantly, until thickened. (The constant stirring is needed to prevent the soup from curdling.) Beat the egg yolks with the sugar in a tureen. Gradually beat in the hot soup. Serve immediately with chopped almonds and cold whipped cream.

Cherry Soup · *Kirsebaersuppe*

Serve it hot as a soup or cold as a dessert.

2 lb. sweet cherries
$3\frac{1}{4}$ pints water
3 oz. sugar, or to taste
1 cinnamon stick
Grated rind of 1 lemon
2 dessertspoons cornflour
4 dessertspoons water
Juice of 1 lemon
$2\frac{1}{2}$ fl. oz. Cherry Heering (optional)
Whipped cream (optional)

Stone cherries and save juice. Reserve 1 cup stoned cherries. Cook remaining cherries and juice in water, with sugar, cinnamon stick, and lemon rind until soft. Remove cinnamon stick. Force through strainer or food mill or purée in blender. Mix cornflour with water to a smooth paste. Stir into soup. Cook 5 minutes or until smooth and thickened, stirring constantly. Stir in lemon juice, Cherry Heering, and reserved cherries. Serve with small almond macaroons. If served as a dessert, top each helping with a spoonful of whipped cream.

Eggs and Pancakes

Danish Custard · *Aeggestand*

Danish menus feature this custard as 'scrambled' eggs when it appears on smørrebrød, smoked salmon, lobster, sweetbreads, or mushrooms, for all of which it is a classic accompaniment.

12 fl. oz. double cream, warmed
4 eggs
¾ teaspoon salt
½ teaspoon white pepper

Combine all ingredients and beat thoroughly. Place in individual baking dishes or a 4- or 6-cup baking-dish. Stand on a rack in a pan of hot water with the water reaching to the level of the mixture. Bake in 325° F., gas mark 3, oven 20 minutes or until firm. Unmould and serve as described above.

Bacon and Egg Omelet · *Flaeskeaeggekage*

One of the few indigenous Danish egg dishes and very tasty.

½ lb. sliced Danish bacon or lean bacon
6 eggs
4 fl. oz. milk or cream
1 dessertspoon flour
½ teaspoon salt
2 dessertspoons chopped chives

Fry bacon in frying-pan until golden brown. Remove and drain. Crumble bacon. Beat egg yolks with milk or cream, flour, salt, and chives. Pour egg mixture into hot bacon fat. Sprinkle crumbled bacon over the top of the omelet when it begins to set. Lift cooked omelet edges with a fork so that the uncooked portion runs underneath. Cook until golden brown and set. Fold and serve hot. Or turn omelet on a plate and replace in frying-pan uncooked side down. Brown lightly and serve.

NOTE: *If the bacon is very fat, pour off all except 3 to 4 dessertspoons fat before cooking omelet.*

Bornholm Omelet

Bornholm is a little paradise of an island that sits rather by itself in the Baltic. It is a famous resort, with unique cliffs and sandy beaches, woods, picturesque little towns – and famous herring, both fresh and smoked.

3 small smoked herring
6 eggs
6 fl. oz. milk or cream
1 teaspoon salt
2 oz. butter
1 cup radish slices
2 cups finely shredded lettuce
2 dessertspoons chopped chives

Bone smoked herring. Beat eggs with milk or cream and salt. Melt butter in a large frying-pan. Add eggs. Cook over low heat, lifting edges of omelet to let uncooked egg run underneath. When omelet is ready to serve, place herring fillets in a star on top of the omelet. Place radish slices between herring fillets in overlapping rows. Sprinkle omelet with lettuce and chives. Serve omelet in pan, steaming hot.

NOTE: *This omelet, which may seem unusual, has an excellent combination of flavours.*

Summer Omelet with Frankfurters

Sommeraeggekage med Pølser

This is a thrifty but pleasant dish, especially when made with the flavourful canned Danish frankfurters that are readily available. What makes it typically Danish is the way the omelet is served.

4 frankfurters, sliced
½ oz. butter
8 eggs
4 fl. oz. milk or cream
Salt
Pepper
2 oz. butter or margarine
Tomatoes
Cucumber
Radishes
Chopped chives

Sauté sliced frankfurters in ½ oz. butter. Beat eggs with milk or cream and season with salt and pepper. Heat 2 oz. butter or margarine in heavy frying-pan. Pour in egg mixture and cook, stirring constantly, until set. Add frankfurter slices and cook until heated through. Place on hot serving dish and surround with sliced tomatoes, sliced cucumber, and radish roses. Sprinkle everything with chopped chives.

Pancakes · *Pandekager*

The Danes are fond of pancakes, and they serve them rolled with a jam filling, or wrapped around a spoonful of ice cream, with powdered sugar sprinkled on top, to go with coffee. Sometimes apples are added to the batter. The following recipe includes beer, which makes for a lighter batter, without affecting the taste of the pancakes.

4 eggs, separated
16 fl. oz. milk
4 fl. oz. mild beer
¼ teaspoon sugar
¼ teaspoon salt
3¾ cups sifted flour

Beat egg yolks thoroughly. Gradually beat in milk, beer, sugar, and salt. Stir in flour. Beat until smooth. Beat egg whites until stiff and fold into batter. Lightly brush a 6-inch frying-pan with butter. Spoon 2 dessertspoons of the batter into the pan and tilt the pan to spread batter evenly over the bottom. Cook over medium heat until golden brown, turn and brown on the other side. Serve hot with strawberry or raspberry jam, or wrap pancakes around a spoonful of ice cream. Sprinkle with powdered sugar.

Variation: Prepare batter as above. Pour 2 tablespoons of batter into frying-pan. Top with one or two pieces of thinly sliced apple. Cover apples with another tablespoon of batter. Fry as directed.

Fish

Boiled Cod or Pike
Baked Cod
Stewed Cod
Fried Eel with Creamed Potatoes
Werner Christiansen's Singapore Eel
Jellied Eel
Curried Fillets of Flounder
Halibut
Fried Herring or Mackerel with Onion Sauce
  Onion Sauce
Mackerel
  Fresh
  Smoked
Steamed Plaice or Flounder
Fried Plaice or Flounder
Plaice Surprise
Boiled Salmon Steaks
Pickled Salmon
Pickled Trout or Mackerel
Werner Christiansen's Fillets of Sole
Jellied Trout with Dill and Lemon
Turbot
Minced White Fish

The Danish Way to Boil Fish

Danish boiled fish can be described only as superb. Of course, the fish itself is excellent, sweet and firm, coming from the cold waters of the north. But the care with which it is prepared has a great deal to do with incomparable end results. Here is a short guide on how to achieve the best results with English fish.

1. Do not wash fish until ready to be cooked.
2. Sprinkle washed and drained fish lightly with salt; let

stand 10 minutes for thin fillets, and up to 1 hour for thicker slices or whole fish.

3. Rinse off fish in cold water and dry.

4. Place fish in cooking utensil and add just enough water to cover. If the fish is in thin slices or fillets, pour the water very gently in order not to damage the fish. Or lower fish into water.

5. The water should be salted – about 1 teaspoon salt for each pint and a half of water. Also, 2 dessertspoons wine vinegar may be added to each pint and a half of water to keep fish extra firm.

6. Preferably use a two-handled rack to boil fish. Place fish on rack and lower into water. This helps avoid damage to the fish. If the fish is large, wrap it in muslin and leave long ends on the cloth. Grasp these ends as you lift the fish in and out of the pan.

7. When boiling fish, the most important point to remember is that the water or liquid that contains the fish must *never* boil or bubble. It must barely simmer – no more.

8. Boil fish covered.

9. Reserve the fish stock for sauces.

10. To cook fish slices or small fish: Place in *boiling* salted water. Lower heat so that water will simmer, not boil. Test fish for doneness with cake tester. It is done when it flakes easily. As soon as fish is done, pour a little cold water into pan to prevent further boiling. Drain thoroughly and serve on clean napkin – this will absorb the excess moisture. Do not cook many slices of fish at one time. If there are many servings, or second helpings, use several pans, saucepans, or deep frying-pans.

To cook large pieces or whole fish: Place in *cold* water and bring quickly to the boil. Reduce heat immediately. Simmer slowly with the lid of the pan partly off so that steam can escape. If the fish is very large, one hour before cooking time make 3 gashes with a sharp knife on each side of the fish. This firms the fish and prevents it from splitting while boiling. Test cooked fish with cake tester for doneness.

11. During boiling, skim with slotted spoon.

12. Even if the fish is to be used cold, remove it from liquid

as soon as it is cooked. If the fish is left to cool in the liquid, it will become waterlogged.

13. Allow 5 to 8 minutes' cooking time per pound of fish, from the moment the cooking liquid reaches the boiling point. Then reduce to a simmer for remaining cooking time. Cooking time depends on the size of fish. The fish is cooked when the flesh flakes easily, or when the bone has loosened itself from the surrounding flesh. Do not overcook fish.

14. For a more firmly fleshed fish, set fish in large bowl, cover with ice cubes, and set under running cold water for 30 minutes. This is good for cod, halibut, bass, and other similar-textured fish, but it should not be applied to delicate fish such as trout.

Boiled Cod or Pike · *Kogt Torsk eller Gedde*

A very fine dish.

Cook fish as in directions immediately preceding. Place drained fish on large platter lined with lettuce leaves. Surround fish with strips of chopped parsley or dill, chopped hard-boiled egg yolks, chopped hard-boiled egg whites, and grated horse-radish. Decorate with parsley or dill sprigs. Serve with melted butter or creamed butter and tiny new potatoes sprinkled with chopped parsley or dill.

Baked Cod

6 slices cod, about ½ to ⅓ inch thick

Sprinkle fish with salt. Let stand in cool place or refrigerator for 1 hour. Wash and dry. Place slices in well-buttered shallow baking-pan. Make following sauce:

2 oz. butter
4 dessertspoons flour
16 fl. oz. fish stock or clam juice
2 egg yolks
2 fl. oz. lemon juice or dry white wine
½ teaspoon salt
¼ teaspoon white pepper
½ cup soft breadcrumbs
2 oz. melted butter

Melt butter. Stir in flour. Gradually stir in fish stock or clam juice. Cook over low heat, stirring constantly, until thick and smooth. Remove from heat and beat in egg yolks, one at a time. Stir in lemon juice or wine, salt, and pepper. Pour sauce over fish slices. Sprinkle with breadcrumbs. Pour melted butter over breadcrumbs. Bake in 400° F., gas mark 6, oven for 20 to 25 minutes or until fish flakes and crumbs are golden brown.

Stewed Cod · *Plukfisk*

Any left-over fish may be used for this dish.

2 oz. butter
4 dessertspoons flour
10 fl. oz. milk or single cream
8 fl. oz. double cream
1 dessertspoon prepared mustard
½ teaspoon salt
1 large onion, thinly sliced
3 cups boiled cod, boned and flaked
3 hard-boiled eggs, cut in wedges
6 slices bread, crustless, toasted and cut into triangles
Parsley sprigs

Melt butter. Stir in flour. Gradually stir in milk and double cream. Cook over low heat, stirring constantly, until smooth and thick. Beat in mustard and salt. Add onion. Simmer, covered, over low heat until onion is tender. Combine fish and sauce. Heat through thoroughly. Pour into serving-dish. Garnish with egg wedges and toast triangles and decorate with parsley sprigs.

NOTE: *1 cup boiled diced potatoes may be added to this dish.*

Fried Eel with Creamed Potatoes
Stegt Aal med Stuvede Kartofler

A classic Danish dish.

3 eels, skinned and cut into 3-inch pieces
Salt
6 oz. flour
2 eggs, beaten
1½ cups fine dry breadcrumbs
5 oz. butter
6 potatoes, peeled and cubed
2 oz. butter
1 oz. flour
16 fl. oz. milk
1 teaspoon salt
½ teaspoon pepper
1 teaspoon grated lemon rind
2 dessertspoons chopped parsley

Sprinkle eel with salt and let stand for 1 hour. Rinse and dry thoroughly. Roll eel pieces in the 1½ cups flour, then in beaten egg, and then in breadcrumbs. Melt 3 oz. butter in a frying-pan. Fry eels, turning occasionally, until golden brown and tender – about 20 minutes. Cook potatoes in boiling salted water until tender. Melt 2 oz. butter. Stir in 1 oz. flour. Add milk gradually. Cook over low flame, stirring constantly, until smooth and thick. Stir in salt, pepper, and lemon rind. Pour sauce over potatoes. Place potatoes in heated serving-dish and surround with fried eel. Sprinkle parsley over potatoes and eel.

Werner Christiansen's Singapore Eel

A superb recipe from the Coq d'Or Restaurant in Copenhagen.

3 lb. fresh eels, cleaned and skinned
2 oz. butter
2 dessertspoons curry powder, or more
1 cup chopped carrots
1 cup chopped celery
1 cup chopped mushrooms
1½ cups skinned, chopped fresh tomatoes
1½ teaspoons salt
¼ teaspoon freshly ground black pepper
4 fl. oz. water or fish stock, or more
8 fl. oz. dry white wine

Cut eels into 1½-inch pieces. Heat butter in deep pan and stir in curry powder. Cook over medium heat 3 minutes, stirring constantly. Add carrots, celery, mushrooms, tomatoes, and stir thoroughly. Add eel, salt and pepper, water or fish stock, and white wine. Simmer, covered, over low heat about 18 to 20 minutes, stirring occasionally. Check for moisture; if too thick, add a little more water or wine. If too thin, thicken with a little flour. Serve with fluffy dry rice.

NOTE: *This dish can also be made with prawns. In this case, the sauce should simmer for about 15 minutes before adding the raw prawns (which have been shelled and deveined) and cooked 7 to 10 minutes longer, depending on the size of the prawns.*

Jellied Eel · *Aal i Gelé*

Serve as a main course with creamed potatoes (see fried eel with creamed potatoes*), or on open-faced sandwiches, or as one of the dishes of the cold table.

2 eels, skinned and cut into 2-inch pieces
1 onion, sliced
2 bay leaves
4 peppercorns
6 cups water
2 dessertspoons wine or tarragon vinegar
2 envelopes unflavoured gelatin
2 fl. oz. water
2 dessertspoons chopped parsley

Combine eels, onions, bay leaves, peppercorns, and water. Bring to the boil and simmer over low heat until eel is tender – about 20 minutes. Remove eel; strain and reserve stock. Cool eel and remove bones. Keep eel in large pieces. Add vinegar to fish stock. Soak gelatin in 2 fl. oz. cold water for 5 minutes. Heat fish stock and stir in gelatin. Cook over low heat until gelatin is completely dissolved. Pour 1 cup liquid into a rinsed 6-cup ring mould. Chill until firm. Place eel pieces in decorative design on gelatin and sprinkle parsley over fish. Pour remaining gelatin over fish. (If there is any stock left over, pour into small rinsed custard cups and serve with other salads.) Chill eel mould until firm. Unmould and decorate with parsley sprigs.

Curried Fillets of Flounder

2 oz. butter
2 dessertspoons grated onion
½ teaspoon salt
⅛ teaspoon white pepper
1 teaspoon mild curry powder
5 fl. oz. white wine
1½ lb. fillets of flounder (or other white fish)
½ oz. flour
4 fl. oz. single cream
2 dessertspoons grated Parmesan cheese

In frying-pan, melt 1 oz. of the butter. Stir in grated onion, salt, pepper, and curry powder. Cook over low heat 3 minutes, stirring constantly. Blend in white wine and bring to the boil. Lower heat, bring liquid to simmer, and poach fish fillets in it, a few at a time. Transfer poached fish to buttered shallow baking-dish. Melt remaining butter in another frying-pan and stir in flour. Gradually stir in single cream and pan dripping from poaching fish. Cook, stirring constantly, over a low flame until thickened and smooth. Pour sauce over fish and sprinkle with grated Parmesan cheese. Cover and bake in 350° F., gas mark 4, oven for about 15 minutes, or until lightly browned. Serve with boiled potatoes and pickled cucumbers.

Halibut · *Helleflynder*

Much eaten in Denmark. Prepare as for cod.

Fried Herring or Mackerel with Onion Sauce

Mackerel can be substituted for herring in this simple and tasty fish dish.

6 medium-sized fresh herring or mackerel
Salt
Pepper
2 oz. flour
2 eggs, well beaten
1½ cups fine dry breadcrumbs
3 oz. butter or margarine

Onion Sauce

3 large onions, sliced
8 fl. oz. water
1 oz. butter
½ oz. flour
6 fl. oz. milk or single cream
6 fl. oz. onion broth
½ teaspoon salt
¼ teaspoon sugar

Remove fish heads. Split and bone the fish. Rinse and pat dry. Sprinkle fish with salt and pepper. Roll fish in flour, then in beaten egg, and last in breadcrumbs. Melt butter in frying-pan and brown fish on both sides. Serve with onion sauce and boiled potatoes.

To make *sauce*, slice onions and cook in water until transparent. Drain and reserve 6 fl. oz. of the liquid. Melt butter. Stir in flour. Add milk and onion broth gradually. Stir in salt and sugar. Cook over low heat, stirring constantly, until smooth and thick. Add onions and heat through thoroughly. Serve over fish.

Mackerel · *Makrel*

A very popular Danish fish.

Fresh mackerel is usually boiled or fried. Before frying, stuff body cavity with a mixture of 3 oz. of butter and 1 cup chopped parsley or dill. Sew opening before cooking.

Smoked mackerel. Cook with skin or without. Cut fish into pieces and pan-fry in a little butter. Serve with scrambled eggs or with boiled vegetables, such as potatoes, cauliflower, green peas, carrots, or asparagus. Decorate with twisted lemon slices.

Steamed Plaice or Flounder

Plaice is a favourite Danish fish, sold at comparatively high prices.

Allow ½ to ¾ pound of fish for each serving. Skin and clean fish and cut into serving pieces. Place into boiling salted water. Simmer until fish flakes. Skim if necessary. Drain thoroughly and serve with melted butter, chopped parsley, and boiled potatoes.

Fried Plaice or Flounder

6 small plaice or flounder, filleted, skinned, cleaned, and cut into serving pieces
Salt
Pepper
1 egg, well beaten
1 cup flour or fine dry breadcrumbs
3 oz. butter

Sprinkle fish with salt and pepper. Dip fillets into egg and roll in flour or breadcrumbs. Heat butter in frying-pan. Fry fish until golden brown. Serve with browned butter and lemon wedges and boiled potatoes. Decorate platter with parsley or dill sprigs.

Plaice Surprise · *Rødspaette Surprise*

This is a spectacular dish Danish cooks seem to turn out easily. In Denmark the fish is fried, but for greater ease of preparation I recommend the baking method. The results are about the same.

1½ lb. whole plaice
2 potatoes, peeled and sliced into finger lengths
Salt
2 oz. flour
1 egg, well beaten
1 cup fine dry breadcrumbs
½ cup salad oil or lard (for frying-pan method) or
¼ lb. butter (for baking method)
1 cup creamed chopped spinach
1 3-oz. jar tiny imported Danish shrimps or ½ cup tiny cooked and shelled fresh shrimps
12 2-inch asparagus tips, cooked (tinned, frozen, or fresh)

Frying-pan method. Skin fish and remove head. Slash fish on one side down the length of the backbone. Strip the fillets partially from the bone. Turn fillets out like lapels. Place raw potatoes into the pocket to hold the fillets in position. Sprinkle fish with salt. Let stand 10 minutes. Rinse fish, remove potatoes, and wipe fish dry. Coat entire fish with flour – including the turned-out fillets and the pocket. Dip fish into beaten egg, coating all the surfaces. Dip into breadcrumbs and coat fish thoroughly. Heat salad oil or lard in a large frying-pan. Fry fish pocket side down until brown, making sure fillets are turned out. Fill pockets in the fish with a strip of creamed spinach, shrimps, and asparagus tips, arranged in a neat, decorative pattern.

Baking method. Prepare fish as above. Melt butter. Brush generously over a flat heatproof serving platter. Place fish on platter. Drip remaining melted butter over the whole fish, coating the entire surface. Hold lapels in place with toothpicks. Bake in 375° F., gas mark 5, oven about 25 minutes or until golden brown and tender. Decorate with spinach, shrimps, and asparagus as described above.

NOTE: *I know that it is difficult to imagine this dish without a picture. What it amounts to is a fish cut open and stuffed with spinach, shrimps, and asparagus, with two flaps at either side. Very colourful and Danish.*

Boiled Salmon Steaks

Allow $\frac{1}{2}$ to $\frac{3}{4}$ pound fish for each serving. Cut salmon into steaks about $\frac{1}{2}$ inch thick. Place salmon steaks in boiling salted water seasoned with 6 peppercorns and 2 bay leaves. Simmer until fish flakes. Remove fish carefully. Drain and serve with hollandaise sauce or melted butter garnished with chopped dill or parsley. For 6 persons, serve 16 fl. oz. hollandaise sauce or 8 fl. oz. melted butter garnished with 2 dessertspoons finely chopped dill or parsley.

Pickled Salmon · *Gravlaks*

Connoisseurs consider *gravlaks* superior to smoked salmon. The dish is an ancient one, of Swedish origin, and easy to make. But it is essential that the salmon be fresh, because fish that has been frozen cannot be used for pickling – the texture would break down. A plentiful supply of fresh dill is also essential.

7 to 8 lb. fresh salmon in one piece, with the bones in
6 oz. salt
$\frac{1}{4}$ lb. sugar
1 dessertspoon whole white pepper, coarsely crushed
1 teaspoon whole allspice, coarsely crushed
6 dessertspoons cognac
2 large bunches fresh dill

Choose middle cut from salmon. Clean fish, leaving skin on, and carefully remove bones so that the two big fillets remain. Rinse under cold water and dry carefully with kitchen towel, taking care that the fish does not break. Mix together salt, sugar, pepper, and allspice. Rub seasonings carefully into all the surfaces of the fish. Sprinkle with cognac. Wash dill and place one third of it in the bottom of a deep pan or bowl (do not use aluminium). Place one piece of salmon, skin side down, on dill. Top fish with another third of dill. Place the second piece of salmon, skin side up, on dill. Cover with the remaining dill. Set heavy plate or board on fish and keep in refrigerator from 24 to 36 hours, preferably the latter. Drain fish, scrape off dill and spices, and slice on the slant, away from the skin. Serve with lemon wedges, mustard sauce,* Danish custard,* and freshly ground pepper. Makes about 15 servings.

NOTE: Gravlaks *may be kept in the refrigerator for one week. In Denmark, the skin of the fish is sliced and fried in butter until crisp. It is then served with the salmon.*

Pickled Trout or Mackerel · *Grav Ørred og Makrel*

These are prepared in the same manner as the salmon. For each pound of fish, use 1 teaspoon salt, ½ teaspoon sugar, ¼ teaspoon white pepper, crushed, and a scant dessertspoon cognac. Omit allspice but use plenty of fresh dill.

Werner Christiansen's Fillets of Sole

From the Coq d'Or Restaurant in Copenhagen.

10 oz. butter
2 dessertspoons lemon juice
1 dessertspoon chopped parsley
½ teaspoon salt
¼ teaspoon white pepper
6 large fillets of sole
2 teaspoons curry powder
1 teaspoon tomato purée
1 dessertspoon chutney
6 slices pineapple, preferably fresh
3 dessertspoons flour
8 fl. oz. fish stock
8 fl. oz. double cream
Salt
Pepper

Brown 4 oz. butter in heavy frying-pan. Stir in lemon juice, parsley, salt, and pepper. Cook for 1 minute. Cook fish in butter mixture until golden brown and flaky. Do not overcook. Place fillets on large hot platter, overlapping slightly. Keep hot. While fish is cooking, melt 4 oz. butter in another frying-pan. Stir in curry powder, tomato purée, and chutney. Cook 3 minutes, stirring constantly. Sauté pineapple in mixture until golden brown. Arrange pineapple slices around fish so that they overlap and keep hot. Make sauce by melting 2 oz. butter. Stir flour and cook, stirring constantly, for about 3 minutes. Do not let brown. Combine fish stock with cream and stir into butter-flour mixture. Cook over low heat until smooth and thickened. Season to taste with salt and pepper. Pour sauce over fish and serve with tiny boiled potatoes.

Jellied Trout with Dill and Lemon
Foreller i Gelé med Citron og Dild

8 fl. oz. dry white wine
1 dessertspoon salt
1 small onion, sliced
6 sprigs fresh dill
32 fl. oz. water
6 small trout or frozen Danish trout, thawed
32 fl. oz. quick aspic*
Sliced truffles

Combine wine, salt, onion, dill, and water in fish cooker or deep frying-pan. Bring to a simmer. Place fish in liquid, preferably on rack. Bring back to simmering, and simmer gently for 5 minutes. Carefully remove fish. Make diagonal slits in fish's skin just below head and above tail and carefully remove skin. Leave heads and tails intact. Place fish on serving platter (preferably a silver one) in orderly rows. Chill. Spoon chilled but still liquid aspic over fish. Make as many layers as desired, chilling after each layer is applied. Decorate fish with sliced truffles and cover with another layer of aspic. Decorate platter with additional chopped aspic, inner leaves of lettuce, lemon twists, and dill sprigs. Serve with sharp mustard sauce.*

Turbot

This excellent fish is greatly prized in Denmark as in England, and in France.

It can be boiled and fried in the same way as plaice* and flounder.*

Minced White Fish · *Fiskefars*

This is the Danish variation of the French fish quenelles or the Jewish gefüllte fish. The dish is very delicate, and there are various ways of making it. Moulded, and accompanied by hollandaise sauce and lobster, prawns, and/or crab meat, it makes an excellent party dish.

1½ lb. skinned, boned, and minced raw cod, haddock, pike, or salmon
1 dessertspoon salt
9 oz. soft butter
3 dessertspoons flour
1 teaspoon white pepper
2 eggs, well beaten
About 8 fl. oz. single cream or milk

Mince fish 4 or 5 times with finest blade of the mincer or pound with potato masher or blend in electric blender, a little at a time. (The fish must be minced this finely, or the dish won't be a success.) Measure 1½ lb. minced fish. Stir salt into fish and beat until very smooth. Cream 6 oz. butter until very soft. Beat in flour and pepper. Add fish and blend until very smooth. Beat in eggs. Gradually beat in cream until mixture is soft and mushy, and about the consistency of thick apple sauce. Melt 3 oz. butter in a heavy frying-pan. Drop in fish mixture by tablespoonfuls and fry gently over medium heat until golden brown on both sides. Serve with any standard mushroom or tomato sauce and boiled potatoes sprinkled with parsley or dill.

To bake in mould: Pour mixture into a well-buttered 2½ pint ring mould or loaf pan. Cover dish with waxed paper or aluminium foil and tie securely. Place mould on a rack in a pan with simmering water. The water should come ⅔ up the mould. Cook for 35 to 45 minutes or until fish tests firm. Do not boil water in pan rapidly, or the fish mould will have holes. Unmould on hot plate. Fill centre with hot lobster, prawns, or crab meat and serve with hollandaise sauce.

Chicken, Duck, Goose, Venison, Game Birds

Chicken with Parsley · *Stegt Kylling*

The Danes usually roast their chickens in a casserole rather than in the oven, the way we do.

1 3- to 4-lb. whole chicken
2 teaspoons salt
½ teaspoon white pepper
3 oz. butter
1½ cups chopped parsley
⅖ pint hot chicken bouillon

Cream Sauce

3 dessertspoons pan drippings
3 dessertspoons flour
8 fl. oz. hot chicken bouillon
5 fl. oz. double cream
Salt
Pepper
1 oz. butter

Rub chicken inside and out with salt and pepper. Combine half of the butter with the chopped parsley. Stuff chicken with mixture; truss. Heat remaining butter in Dutch oven or casserole. Brown chicken in it on all sides. Add hot bouillon. Simmer, covered, 50 minutes to 1 hour or until chicken is tender. Transfer chicken to serving-dish and keep hot. Pour chicken stock from Dutch oven into measuring cup, leaving 3 dessertspoons in the Dutch oven. Add enough hot bouillon to make 8 fl. oz. To make *sauce*, heat the 3 dessertspoons pan drippings in Dutch oven. Stir in flour and cook over medium heat until golden, stirring constantly. Add hot chicken bouillon and cook until thick and smooth. Reduce heat to lowest possible and stir in cream. Season with salt and pepper to taste. Heat through thoroughly without boiling. Remove from heat and beat in butter, beating vigorously until butter is absorbed. To serve, decorate with lettuce leaves, sliced tomatoes, and parsley sprigs. Serve sauce separately and accompany chicken with browned potatoes and a tossed green salad.

Chicken with Prawns and Asparagus

Kyllinger med Rejer og Asparges

This recipe comes from the Countess Ella Bille Brahe Selby, who lives in her ancestral home of Steensgaard in Funen. This enchanting sixteenth-century manor house is the kind of place where you would like to be eighteen and in love.

2 chickens, about 1½ to 2 lb. each
Chicken bouillon
4 oz. butter
Salt
Pepper
¼ cup each chopped onion, celery, carrot, and parsley
4 dessertspoons flour
1 8-oz. can white asparagus
2 egg yolks
4 fl. oz. double cream
½ lb. cooked, shelled, and deveined prawns or shrimps, or 1 8-oz. can, drained

Place whole chickens in a deep pan. Add chicken bouillon, 2 oz. butter, salt and pepper to taste, and chopped vegetables. Simmer, covered, over low heat until chickens are tender, or about 30 to 40 minutes. Remove chickens from broth. Reserve and strain broth. Cool chickens and cut them in half. Take out the bones, or cut chickens into serving pieces. Place in serving dish and keep hot. Drain asparagus and reserve liquid. Reduce chicken broth and asparagus liquid to make about 18 fl. oz. liquid in all. Melt 2 oz. butter and stir in flour. Add chicken-asparagus liquid and cook over low heat, stirring constantly, until smooth and thick. Beat together egg yolks and cream. Stir into sauce. Heat sauce through but do not boil. Pour sauce over chicken. Garnish with prawns or shrimps and asparagus. Serve with boiled potatoes or rice.

NOTE: *When this dish is made with the white Danish asparagus, it is a charming white and pink creation.*

Mrs A. W. Nielsen's Chicken à la King
Kylling à la King

Mrs A. W. Nielsen, a famous Copenhagen hostess, served this to me accompanied with yellow saffron rice and a tossed green salad. The whole thing looked lovely.

The butter, added to the broth in which the chicken breasts are cooked, helps to keep them juicy.

6 whole chicken breasts, skinned and boned
1½ pints chicken bouillon, boiling
5 oz. butter
4 dessertspoons flour
Salt
Pepper
4 fl. oz. double cream
¾ lb. sliced mushrooms, sautéed in a little butter
12 strips red pimento, about ¼ inch × 2½ inches
3 medium-sized truffles (optional)

Place chicken breasts in Dutch oven or heavy casserole. Cover with boiling chicken bouillon. Add 3 oz. butter. Simmer, covered, over low heat for about 30 minutes or until breasts are tender. Drain, reserve stock, and keep chicken breasts hot. Skim fat off stock and measure 1½ pints. Heat stock. Melt 2 oz. butter and stir in flour. Gradually add the

$1\frac{1}{2}$ pints hot chicken stock. Cook, stirring constantly, until sauce is thickened and smooth. Season with salt and pepper to taste. Remove from heat and stir in cream. Add mushrooms to sauce. Heat through thoroughly without boiling. Place chicken breasts on a large platter and coat with a little of the sauce. Decorate with pimento strips and truffles. The truffles may be cut into decorative patterns with truffle cutters or chopped fine. Garnish with lettuce leaves and surround with mounds of yellow saffron rice. Serve remaining sauce separately. Or heat chicken breasts in the whole of the sauce and serve in a deep dish, with a side dish of yellow saffron rice.

Brown Chicken Fricassee with Madeira

1 4-lb. chicken, cut in pieces
2 oz. flour
1 teaspoon salt
$\frac{1}{4}$ teaspoon pepper
3 oz. butter
1 medium-sized onion, sliced
24 fl. oz. hot chicken bouillon
8 fl. oz. madeira
2 bay leaves
6 fl. oz. double cream

Coat chicken on all sides with flour seasoned with salt and pepper. Shake off excess flour. Heat 2 oz. butter in heavy frying-pan. Brown chicken in it on all sides. The chicken should be the colour of dark wood. Transfer chicken pieces to casserole. Brown onion in remaining pan juices. Add onion to chicken, together with hot chicken bouillon, madeira, and bay leaves. Bring to the boil. Simmer, covered, over low heat until chicken is tender, from 45 minutes to 1 hour. Remove chicken to heated serving platter and keep hot. Over high heat, boil sauce down to 2 cups. Strain sauce, heat again. Stir in cream and 1 oz. butter. Heat thoroughly but do not boil. Pour over chicken pieces. Serve fricassee surrounded with sautéed mushrooms, halved grilled tomatoes, small mounds of buttered peas, and browned potatoes. Makes about 4 servings.

Roast Duck with Apples and Prunes · *Stegt And*

Roast duck is an all-year favourite in Denmark. Restaurants serve it in many French versions, such as duck with oranges or duck with cherries. A very good way is to prepare it stuffed with apples and prunes, the way it is served in Danish homes and restaurants.

Allow 1 to 1½ lb. of duck for each serving.

1 5- to 6-lb. duck
½ lemon
Salt
Pepper
⅔ to 1 cup tart apples, cored and chopped
⅔ to 1 cup soaked prunes, stoned and chopped
½ oz. butter
1 dessertspoon flour
2 dessertspoons red currant jelly

Remove all excess fat from the duck; much of it is concentrated around the openings. Reserve some fat. Rub duck inside and out with lemon, salt, and pepper. Combine chopped apples and chopped prunes. Stuff duck. Sew or skewer opening and truss in the usual manner. Rub duck with fat and prick all over lightly with fork to allow excess fat to escape during roasting. Place duck on rack in shallow roasting-pan. Preheat oven to 450° F., gas mark 8. Place duck in oven and reduce heat to 350° F., gas mark 4. Roast about 25 minutes to the pound or until tender. Pour off fat as it accumulates in pan. Baste occasionally. Remove duck to large hot platter. Remove trussing string and skewers. Keep hot. Pour all fat from roasting-pan. Add enough water to make 1 cup; heat. Cream butter and flour together. Stir into hot liquid in pan until butter is melted and sauce thickened. Stir in red currant jelly. Serve sauce separately. Garnish duck with poached apple halves* stuffed with prunes in port wine.* Decorate with parsley and lettuce leaves. Serve with red cabbage* or pickled beets* and sugar-browned potatoes.*

Roast Duck with Parsley Stuffing

Proceed as for roast duck with apples and prunes,* but for the apples and prunes substitute a stuffing made from 3 oz. butter and 2 cups finely chopped parsley, creamed together. Since this is a rich stuffing, make sure to remove every trace of excess fat from duck before cooking.

Make gravy by substituting single cream for half of the water and omitting red currant jelly. Add minced liver and heart to gravy and simmer about 2 or 3 minutes without boiling. Correct seasonings.

Serve with boiled potatoes sprinkled with chopped parsley and buttered green peas.

Mrs A. W. Nielsen's Pickled Duck · *Krydret And*

This excellent dish may also be made with wild duck, pheasant, or grouse.

3 pints water
2 oz. salt
5 bay leaves
8 whole peppercorns
1 carrot, sliced
1 medium-sized onion, stuck with 3 whole cloves
8 fl. oz. vinegar
1 or 2 whole wild duck, cleaned for cooking

Combine all ingredients except duck. Place duck in marinade. Let stand in cool place 2 days. Simmer duck until tender; the time depends on the duck's age. Drain duck and reserve marinade. Bone duck and cut into strips. Place in deep bowl and add marinade to cover. Press down with a weighted plate. Let stand overnight. Drain and dry. Serve with yellow pea soup* or with creamed potatoes and a salad.

Roast Goose with Apples and Prunes
Gaasesteg med Aebler og Svesker

The traditional Christmas bird, eaten on Christmas Eve – and throughout the winter and most of the summer. The flocks of snowy geese in the farmyards are one of the prettiest sights of Denmark.

However, know your goose before you cook it. Unless it is under ten months old, it is apt to be tough and should not be roasted but braised. If you can't determine the age of your bird, go by the weight and braise every one that weighs over 10 pounds.

Since geese are very fat, it is imperative to prick the skin of a goose frequently and lightly to allow excess fat to escape – else it will taste greasy. Pre-roasting the bird in a very hot oven also helps get rid of the excess fat that has put off many people from enjoying a goose, one of the best birds when well cooked. The stuffing of a goose is also apt to be overpowered by fat, and I recommend discarding it. Instead, use apples and prunes cooked separately to achieve more of the excellent flavour combination. (The taste of the stuffing will have penetrated the bird's flesh during cooking time.)

Allow about 1 to 1½ pounds goose for each serving, and allow about ½ cup stuffing to each pound of bird.

P.S. It really *is* worth while to cook a goose in the Danish manner.

1 7- to 8-lb. young goose, ready to cook
½ lemon
Salt
Pepper
2 cups tart apples, cored and chopped
2 cups soaked prunes, stoned and chopped
1 oz. butter
2 dessertspoons flour
⅓ cup red currant jelly (optional)

Wash goose with hot water inside and out and dry. Trim off excess fat, and reserve it. Rub with lemon inside and out. Sprinkle inside and out with salt and pepper. Combine apples and prunes and stuff goose. Sew or skewer opening and truss in the usual manner. Prick goose all over lightly with fork to allow excess fat to escape during roasting. Rub goose on all sides with reserved goose fat. Place on rack in shallow roasting pan on one side. Pre-heat oven to 450° F., gas mark 8. Place goose in oven and turn down heat to 350° F., gas mark 4. Roast about 20 to 25 minutes to the pound. Pour off fat as it accumulates in pan. Baste goose occasionally. After the first hour turn the bird on the other side. Roast the goose for the last 15 minutes on its back so that the breast will brown. Test for doneness by moving legs up and down – they should move easily. Remove goose to large hot platter. Remove trussing string and skewers. Keep goose hot. Pour all fat from roasting-pan. Add enough water to make 16 fl. oz.; heat. Cream butter and flour together. Stir into hot liquid in pan until butter is melted and sauce thickened. Stir in red currant jelly. Serve sauce separately.

Dish up goose with poached apple halves* stuffed with prunes in port wine.* Arrange these around goose. Decorate with parsley and lettuce leaves. Serve with red cabbage* Danish style and sugar-browned potatoes.*

Giblet Ragout · *Kraaseragout*

Some supermarkets and poultry dealers sell giblets separately. Otherwise, freeze giblets after cooking a goose or duck until you have accumulated a sufficient amount.

6 duck or goose giblets (6 hearts, 6 gizzards, 6 livers)
2 oz. flour
2 oz. butter
1 large onion, grated
3 carrots, diced
1 teaspoon salt
½ teaspoon paprika
½ teaspoon curry powder
1 teaspoon gravy colouring
Water
2½ fl. oz. sherry or madeira

Clean giblets. Scald by pouring boiling water over them. Cut them in half. Coat pieces with flour. Melt butter in saucepan. Add giblets, grated onion and carrots. Cook over medium heat until golden brown, stirring frequently. Add salt, paprika, curry powder, gravy colouring, and enough water to cover. Simmer, covered, over low heat until giblets are tender. Add sherry or madeira and heat through thoroughly. Serve with mashed potatoes and a green salad.

NOTE: *I presume this recipe could be applied to chicken giblets, though I have not tried it.*

Poached Apple Halves

A garnish for roast goose and roast duck.

4 medium-sized baking apples
4 oz. sugar
8 fl. oz. water

Pare and core apples. Cut into halves horizontally. Boil together sugar and water for 3 minutes. Lower heat. Add apple halves slowly. (Cook only a few pieces at a time.) Simmer in gently boiling syrup until tender; test with a straw or cake tester. Do not overcook. Carefully lift out apple halves with slotted spoon. Keep hot. Fill hollows with cooked, stoned prunes. Serve hot with roast goose* or roast duck.*

Prunes in Port Wine

A garnish for roast goose and roast duck.

½ lb. prunes
Cold water
3 dessertspoons sugar (optional)
Port wine, sherry, or madeira

Cover prunes with cold water and bring to the boil. Drain. Add sugar and enough wine to cover prunes. Simmer over low heat about 15 to 20 minutes or until prunes are tender but still firm. Cool in wine. At serving time, drain prunes and stone them. The stones may be replaced by blanched almonds or walnut halves.

Venison, Hare and Game Birds
Vildt og Fuglevildt

The idyllic Danish forests, where in spring the dappled sunlight streams on the ground, carpeted with white anemones, are the home of much game. There are deer, hare, and even boar, and many game birds, such as pheasant, partridge, quail, grouse, snipe, woodcock, and others. They seem very tame to us; driving through the quiet Danish country lanes, you see many of the birds and their young foraging in the fields, unafraid of man. And in the rushes around the edges of Denmark's lakes, many wild ducks are shot in their season. Wise forestry planning, planned restocking, and moderate sportsmen have made Denmark into a country where centuries of hunting have not worked havoc.

The Danes prize venison and game birds, both as sport and eating, and they also prepare them extremely well. Venison is carefully larded, either by the butcher who sells it, or at home, and game birds are barded, or covered with sheets of lard or other pork fat, to insure juiciness during the cooking process, an essential step in the preparation of meats that are essentially dry and overlean.

Venison, cooked in the Danish manner, may be marinated and then slowly pot-roasted or oven-roasted, and finished with a cream sauce. Or sweet or sour cream may be added during the pot-roasting. Game birds are pot-roasted or oven-roasted, and also cooked with cream or finished with a cream sauce. The sauces are often made more delicious by the addition of sautéed mushrooms. Sugar-browned potatoes* and red currant jelly are traditional accompaniments. Juniper berries are a favourite flavouring.

Traditional Danish cooking also includes many very beautiful and rather complicated dishes for making game salmis, terrines, aspics, and other *pièces montées*. These are really French recipes and relics of the French haute cuisine that radiated from the French courts of the Golden Age to the court and the noble households of Denmark.

Basically, venison and game birds are eaten for their own distinctive taste rather than for fancy garnishes. The problem is to get them tender and juicy, and there really is no other way, in Denmark or anywhere else, of doing this, than by the methods described.

How to Lard Venison or Other Meat

Many butchers, if given advance notice, will lard meat. Otherwise, larding can be done in the home kitchen, since it is but a method by which strips of salt pork or bacon, called lardoons, are inserted into lean meat to give it the fat content necessary for tenderness in cooking, as well as additional juiciness and flavour.

Larding is most easily done with a larding needle, which may be bought in good household stores. If none is available, an ice pick, a skewer, or a knitting needle can be pressed into service.

Make lardoons by cutting salt pork or bacon into 2- or 3-inch-long strips about $\frac{1}{4}$ inch thick for big cuts of meat, such as venison, or $\frac{1}{8}$ inch thick for small pieces and birds. If the pork is excessively salty, blanch and dry it before using. (Blanching salt pork is done by placing the salt pork in cold water, bringing it slowly to a boil, and simmering it a few minutes, depending on the quantity of pork to be blanched. The salt pork is then drained and plunged into cold water.)

Allow 3 ounces of fat for each pound of lean meat and increase the amount if the meat is very tough and dry.

If you have no larding needle, push an ice-pick, a skewer, or a knitting needle through the meat, making deep holes about 1 to 2 inches apart. Do this neatly, for the lardoons will show in the carved meat. Push the lardoons through these holes with the ice-pick, the skewer, or the knitting needle you have been using.

Many cooks rub the lardoons with garlic, herbs, or spices, such as cloves or cinnamon, to give their meats additional flavour, or they marinate them in brandy.

The lardoons cook into the meat and should not be removed before serving.

When larding a bird, use thin lardoons and place them at right angles to the breastbone.

Venison Steaks with Blue Cheese

Dyresteg med Danablu

1 onion, chopped
1 carrot, chopped
2 bay leaves
½ teaspoon pepper
16 fl. oz. dry white wine
4 fl. oz. vinegar
2 fl. oz. water
4 venison steaks, about ½ lb. each
4 oz. butter
8 fl. oz. double cream
½ cup (about 2 oz.) Danish Blue cheese, crumbled

Combine onion, carrot, bay leaves, pepper, wine, vinegar, and water and bring to the boil. Cool and pour into deep bowl (do not use aluminium). Place venison steaks in marinade and refrigerate for 24 hours. Remove from marinade and dry. Heat butter in large skillet and sauté steaks in it until browned on both sides. They should be on the rare side. Place steaks on heated serving-platter. Stir cream and Danish Blue cheese into pan drippings and cook over lowest possible heat until sauce is smooth. Pour over steaks. In Denmark, this was served with boiled potatoes, browned potatoes, red cabbage,* and a garnish of red currant jelly.

Roast Loin of Venison · *Stegt Dyreryg*

The Danes prefer to roast the loin of deer and to pot roast the haunch. Both cuts must be larded before using. The following recipe may also be used for a saddle or a leg of venison.

1 loin of venison, about 5 pounds
Fat pork for larding
1½ teaspoons salt
½ teaspoon pepper
½ lb. butter, melted
8 fl. oz. hot bouillon
8 fl. oz. hot dry red or white wine or 8 fl. oz. hot bouillon
12 fl. oz. pan dripping
½ oz. flour
4 fl. oz. double cream
2–3 oz. currant jelly
2 fl. oz. madeira (optional)

Lard* meat. Rub with salt and pepper. Brush with melted butter. Preheat oven to 325° F., gas mark 3. Place meat on rack in shallow baking-pan. Add hot bouillon and hot wine. Roast about 2½ hours, or until meat is tender, allowing 25 to 30 minutes to the pound. Baste frequently with pan juices; if necessary, add a little more hot bouillon and wine. Remove meat to hot platter and keep hot. Skim off fat from pan juices and measure 12 fl. oz. (If necessary, add hot bouillon to make up measure.) Stir flour with a little water into a smooth paste. Heat pan juices and stir in flour. Cook, stirring constantly, until thick and smooth. Remove from heat. Stir in cream, currant jelly, and madeira. Heat through but do not boil. Serve venison garnished with additional currant jelly, chestnut purée, and a chicory salad. Serve sauce separately.

Pot-Roasted Venison or Hare

The idea is to tenderize the meat before cooking it.

1 5- to 6-lb. haunch of venison, or 1 5- to 6-lb. hare
Fat pork for larding
Water
Dry red wine
1 onion, sliced
1 bay leaf
6 juniper berries
6 peppercorns
2½ oz. butter
16 fl. oz. hot beef bouillon or ⅖ pint beef bouillon and ⅖ pint marinade
12 fl. oz. pan juices
½ oz. flour
4 fl. oz. cream
1 dessertspoon grated orange rind (optional)

Lard* meat or hare. Place in a deep bowl (do not use aluminium) and cover with equal quantities of water and dry red wine. Add onion, bay leaf, juniper berries, and peppercorns. Marinate in a cool place overnight or up to 6 days, depending on age of meat. Drain; reserve marinade. Dry. Heat 2 oz butter in Dutch oven and brown meat in it. Lower heat and add beef bouillon. Simmer, covered, until meat is tender; this depends on the age of the meat. Place meat on serving platter and keep hot. Measure 12 fl. oz. of the pan juices and heat. Knead together flour and ½ oz. butter and stir into pan juices until butter is melted and sauce thickened. Stir in cream and orange rind. Heat through but do not boil. Slice meat and pour a little of the gravy over the slices. Serve remainder separately. Garnish platter with parsley sprigs and orange or lemon cups filled with red currant jelly. Serve with sugar-browned potatoes* and any buttered vegetables.

Variation: The venison or hare, provided they are young and tender, may be marinated overnight in beer or milk. When ready to cook, drain and dry. Discard beer or milk. Substitute cream or milk for beef bouillon, or use an equal mixture of bouillon and cream. Omit orange rind in sauce seasoning and use, if desired, ⅛ teaspoon nutmeg or allspice instead.

Smothered Hare in Cream · *Haresteg med Fløde*

Danish hare is practically all dark meat and a delicacy.

1 hare, prepared for cooking and cut into pieces
Flour
Salt
Pepper
1½ oz. butter
⅓ cup cognac
1 small onion, minced
2 fl. oz. vinegar
Double cream

Coat hare with flour mixed with salt and pepper. Heat butter in deep pan or casserole and brown hare in it on all sides. Add cognac and flame. When flame has died down, add onion, vinegar, and cream to cover. Simmer, covered, over lowest possible heat (or in 300° F., gas mark 2, oven) until hare is tender, 1¼ hours or more. Serve with puff paste patties filled with red currant jelly, potato croquettes, and a salad.

Game Pâté · *Fuglevildt Postej*

This recipe was developed by Mr Craig Claiborne, the distinguished food editor of the *New York Times* and an admirer of fine Danish cooking. Crisp French bread and a light Bordeaux wine should be served with it.

1 lb. boned pheasant, wild duck, quail, snipe, or other game bird, including the liver, diced
2 truffles, coarsely chopped
¼ cup cognac
Salt
Freshly ground pepper
1 oz. butter
½ cup minced shallots
¾ lb. finely minced veal
¾ lb. finely minced lean pork
½ lb. finely minced salt pork
½ cup fresh shelled pistachio nuts (optional)
4 fl. oz. madeira or cognac
2 eggs
½ teaspoon thyme
½ teaspoon allspice
1 clove garlic, crushed
About 4 thin slices salt pork or bacon
1 bay leaf

Combine game, truffles, and 2 fl. oz. cognac in a bowl. Season with salt and pepper. Refrigerate for at least 1 hour. Melt butter and cook shallots in it for 5 minutes. Combine shallots, minced meats, pistachio nuts, 4 fl. oz. madeira or cognac, eggs, thyme, allspice, and garlic in a bowl. Drain liquid from game and add to mixture. Beat thoroughly with a wooden spoon. Simmer pork or bacon slices for 5 minutes in water. Drain and dry between paper towels. Line the bottom and sides of a 1½-pint baking-dish or pâté mould with a thin layer of the pork or bacon slices. Reserve remaining slices. Divide the minced meat mixture into three parts. Spoon one part into the baking-dish. Cover with half of the marinated game. Add another third of the minced meat mixture and top with remaining game. Add the remaining meat. Place bay leaf on top and cover with remaining pork or bacon slices. Cover with aluminium foil. Set the baking-dish in a larger pan with boiling water half-way up the sides of the baking-dish. Bake in 325° F., gas mark 3, oven 1½ hours, or until pâté has shrunk slightly from the edge of the dish. Remove the pâté from the oven, leaving the baking-dish in the larger pan. Top the pâté with a pan or a dish that fits the top. Fill with canned foods or other weights. Do not remove until the pâté is completely cooled. Refrigerate until ready to serve. Makes about 15 servings.

How to Bard Birds

Barding is a method by which lean fowl, such as game birds, are wrapped with salt pork or bacon before cooking. (Meat is also sometimes barded.) The salt pork or bacon is discarded after cooking.

Barding is much used in Danish game bird cookery, and standard Danish cookbooks invariably instruct how to do it.

For each bird, 4 pieces of salt pork or bacon are necessary. Each piece should be about ¼ inch thick and measure approximately 3 to 4 inches square (or more, depending on the size of the bird). If too salty, the pork should be blanched first, as described in 'How to Lard Venison or Other Meat'.*

Truss bird before barding. Slip 1 piece of salt pork or bacon on either side between the leg and the breast of the bird. Cover the bird, legs and all surfaces, with remaining 2 pieces of salt pork or bacon. Tie with white string 2 or 3 times, so that fat will not be displaced during cooking. Make sure that all the surfaces of the bird are covered with fat.

Pot-Roasted Partridge or Grouse with Mushrooms

Stegt Agerhøne eller Hjerpe med Champignons

This recipe applies to all game birds, though the quantities of cream and mushrooms used depend on the size and number of the birds. It is also a good way of cooking our domestic Cornish game hens.

6 partridge or grouse, ready to cook
Salt
Pepper
12 slices bacon
16 fl. oz. double cream
1 4-oz. can sliced mushrooms or 1 cup sautéed sliced mushrooms

Wash birds. Dry and sprinkle inside and out with salt and pepper. Bard* birds or wrap 2 bacon slices over each breast, tying bacon in place with string. Heat large frying-pan or Dutch oven. Brown birds on all sides. Add cream and mushrooms. Simmer, tightly covered, over low heat for 30 minutes or until birds are tender. Remove barding or bacon before serving. Place on large serving dish and cover with pan gravy. Surround birds with mounds of browned onions and potatoes and sautéed whole mushroom caps and serve with a tossed salad.

Pot-Roasted Pheasant with Grapes
Stegt Fasan med Druer

One of the simplest and best ways of cooking this noble bird.

2 pheasants, ready to cook
2 cups stemmed blue or green grapes
2 oz. flour
3 oz. butter
8 fl. oz. hot chicken bouillon or game stock
1 teaspoon salt
3 dessertspoons madeira, or more

Stuff pheasant with grapes. Tie or skewer openings. Coat birds with flour. Melt butter in Dutch oven. Brown birds on all sides. Add hot chicken bouillon. Simmer, tightly covered, for about 45 minutes, or until birds are tender. Sprinkle with salt. Place pheasant on hot serving-dish; keep hot. Reduce pan juices to about 5 fl. oz. by boiling uncovered. Stir in madeira. Pour gravy over pheasant. Serve garnished with additional blue or green grapes.

Wild Duck · *Vildaender*

The flavour and tenderness of wild duck depend greatly on what they have been feeding on and on their age. There really isn't very much the possessor of wild ducks can do about that except cook them accordingly.

Wild duck are not usually stuffed, but if you suspect that they are too gamey, it is advisable to rub their cavities with lemon or a little ginger, and to stuff them with either chopped celery, apples, or onions, or a combination of these. The stuffing will absorb some of the gamey flavour. It is discarded at serving time.

Before cooking wild duck or other wild birds, make sure that all shot has been removed (it might cost you a tooth), that all meat near the shot or dog-damaged area has been cut away (it might be discoloured and spoiled), and that all the pin-feathers are off. Contrary to English practice, the Danes soak their duck in salted water with a little baking soda for a couple of hours.

The usual way of cooking wild duck in Denmark, where it is a very popular dish, is to pot-roast it.

2 2-lb. wild ducks, ready to cook
Salt
1 cup flour
4 oz. butter
Boiling single cream
3 slices firm rye bread (crusts removed), cubed
2 dessertspoons mango chutney

Sprinkle ducks with salt inside and out. Coat them on all sides with flour.

Heat butter in Dutch oven. Brown duck on all sides. Add enough boiling cream to cover. Simmer, covered, over low heat 45 minutes, or until birds are almost tender. Remove cover and simmer for additional 20 minutes. Remove duck to hot serving-platter. Add cubed rye bread to pan juices and cook, stirring constantly, until sauce is thickened. Stir in chutney. Carve duck and cover pieces with a little of the sauce; serve the rest separately. Garnish serving-platter with sautéed mushroom caps, tiny green peas cooked with butter and a little cream, and mounds of red currant jelly.

Meats

BEEF

Boneless Birds
Minced Beefsteak
Beef Stew with Bacon and Asparagus
Simple Beef Stew
Parsley Hearts
Tongue
Kirsten Christiansen's Potted Liver
Danish Hash
Danish Delight
Curried Oxtail
Forcemeat Balls
Margrethe Schanne's Hamburger

VEAL

Rosalie Holmes's Easter Veal
Kirsten Christiansen's Modern Fricandeau
Mock Chicken
Wiener Schnitzel
Veal Tournedos
Sailor's Stew
Danish Meat Balls
Meat Balls in Celery Sauce
Kidney Stew with Cocktail Sausages and Scrambled Eggs
Braised Calf's Heart
Mock Turtle
Stuffed Cabbage
Stuffed Cauliflower

LAMB

Lamb with Dill
Whitsuntide Lamb

PORK

HAM

Meat

Denmark is a meat-eating country, which is hardly surprising considering she's one of the world's largest exporters of high-grade livestock products. Danish meat is excellent, thanks to the country's extremely advanced methods of animal husbandry. Pedigree stock is raised by farmers trained in the latest agricultural methods, and like royal nurselings, their animals are supervised in life and after by any number of eagle-eyed specialists from the Agricultural Marketing Board and other government agencies. This care is understandable because agricultural products average nearly two-thirds of the value of all Danish exports. Without them, the country could not live, since she has no resources but her soil and her people.

Pork and beef are the chief meats eaten in Denmark, followed by veal and lamb. The latter, young and tender, is a great delicacy, and served as a roast when your hostess wishes to honour you. Veal, too, is far tenderer and more delicate than ours. It is roasted on top of the stove, or turns up as the ubiquitous cutlet, breaded or unbreaded, and often lavishly garnished with fried eggs, anchovies, and capers. Beef, from the black and white and from the red cows that are an integral part of the Danish landscape, is good, but not as good as the best English beef since Danish cows are raised for milk and cream rather than meat.

Danish housewives are very thrifty with their meat, as proved by the endless variety of minced and ground meat dishes. *Hakkebøf* (hamburger) and *frikadeller* (Danish meat balls) are national institutions, especially the latter. The characteristic of Danish minced meat dishes (and of all Scandinavian ones as well, including the famous Swedish meat balls) is that the meat is minced extremely fine, far finer than ordinary English meat. I've found that our butchers will seldom, if ever, mince the meat finely enough for success, and therefore I grind my mince, with an electric grinder.

The Danes are lavish with pork, either fresh or cured. Their way of cutting pork and other meats resembles the English way, so that many of the Danish pork recipes can be reproduced in this country. One of the best is the excellent Danish way of roasting fresh pork, which results in a deliciously crisp skin. The luscious pork dishes served with sauces as well as the pork cooked with prunes in a typical Scandinavian way have met with enthusiastic approval by all the people I've cooked them for. Danish ham, pork loin, sausages, luncheon meat, and bacon are imported into England on a large scale, to the delight of anybody who likes very lean and well-flavoured pork. Since I'd been an aficionado of Danish pork in cans for a long time, and since I like and admire the pig as an animal, I spent quite a lot of time looking at pigs when I was in Denmark.

I can only report that, among the Danes, pigs is not pigs. All 9,000,000 of them (about twice as many as Danes) are, one could say, the triumph of mind over matter, so scientifically have they been bred. They belong to the Landrace breed, lean and streamlined beauties all. Their back fat has been reduced, their bellies are thicker, their hams are larger, and their length has been increased for better bacon. So scientific is the Danish attitude to their bread and butter export that the four large pig experimental stations in the country function in the same manner in every detail to make the experiments as foolproof as possible. All the buildings even turn exactly east to west in case the position in relation to the four points of the compass should have an influence on the pigs.

Denmark is a country of small and medium farms farmed by their owners, and that's where the pigs come from. The pigs of farmer Johannes Horneman Jensen, in the village of Guldbjerg on the island of Funen, are typical of Danish pigdom. Their house, which I cannot bring myself to call a sty, is off one of the four wings enclosing a cobbled farmyard that opens to the road with a deep portal. The farm is a typical traditional Danish farm of half-timbered stone, whitewashed to dazzling brightness under the thick and steep thatched roofs. Mr Jensen also raises cows and chickens and he grows the animals' feed, all in a most efficient modern manner since he has been to agricultural college like most of the young Danish farmers, and married a wife who is a trained home economist. His house, in one of the four wings of the farm complex (the others are barns and machine sheds), is pretty much like a Midwestern farm home, once you're inside, though the kitchen has fewer and simpler appliances.

To come back to the pigs, which the farmer described with the Danish equivalent of being the apple of his eye. Each of them (of various sizes) reposed in a stall of his own, on hay spread fresh daily on a cement floor that drains itself in some way or other; they quenched their thirst from running water. They lived largely on barley and skim milk, fetched fresh every day from the near-by cooperative dairy, for in Denmark dairy by-products are part of the pigs' diet.

Even on his way to becoming ham, bacon, and whatnot (which happens when a pig is about six months old and weighs something around 200 pounds on the hoof) the Danish pig is strictly controlled by a paternal government. Government vets look at him when he turns up live at the slaughterhouse and when he goes to the meat plant, and this is just the beginning of the quality control by the government that keeps the quality of Danish exports so uniformly excellent.

The Danes use their meats differently from English people. Big oven roasts and thick steaks are not common. They are not part of the traditional eating patterns of the country and besides, meat, with the exception of pork, is not inexpensive at all in Denmark. With imagination and thrift, different kinds of meats are combined in one dish and stretched with bacon in a way that is very different from ours. Head, heart, tongue, and tail are used to make surprisingly tasty dishes. Sausages of all kinds abound – another example of the thrift of Danish meat cookery. I think them on the bland side, especially the white favourites called *magisterpølse*, the thought of which gives Danes abroad acute attacks of nostalgia.

The Danes like their meat cooked with a sauce. Plain grilled meat is not part of Danish family cooking, but rather a feature of the French rotisserie kind of restaurant that is becoming fashionable among sophisticated eaters. As seen in the recipes that follow, meat cookery is all – or practically all – very good, and very rich.

Beef

Boneless Birds · *Benløse Fugle*

The Danish version of beef rolls, and an admirable simple dish. The bacon should be full-flavoured, like the Danish.

12 pieces of round or flank steak, 3 × 4 inches, about ½ inch thick
½ teaspoon pepper
12 slices lean bacon or canned Danish bacon
¾ cup chopped parsley
3 oz. flour
3 oz. butter
12 fl. oz. hot bouillon or water
4 fl. oz. dry white or red wine
8 fl. oz. double cream

Pound meat thin. Keep in one piece and avoid making holes. Sprinkle with pepper. Cut bacon to fit size of meat slices. Place a slice of bacon on each slice of meat. Top with 1 tablespoon parsley. Roll meat and tie with string. Coat with flour. Heat butter in frying-pan and brown beef rolls on all sides. Lower heat and add hot bouillon or water and wine. (Or add 16 fl. oz. bouillon instead of wine.) Simmer, covered, over low heat about 1¼ hours or until beef rolls test tender. Place rolls on heated serving platter and keep hot. Add cream to pan liquid and simmer, uncovered, to desired consistency for sauce. Or thicken with a little flour mixed with water to a smooth paste. Pour sauce over rolls or serve separately. Serve with tiny boiled potatoes sprinkled with dill, and buttered carrots and peas. Garnish platter with slices of dill pickle and tomato wedges.

NOTE: *1 medium-sized onion, minced or grated, may be added to or substituted for the parsley.*

Minced Beefsteak · *Hakkebøf*

Danish humorists say that this is the dish all Danes sigh for when abroad.

1½ lb. round steak, minced
1 teaspoon salt
¼ teaspoon pepper
3 oz. flour
2 oz. butter
4 medium-sized onions, sliced
6 fried eggs

Combine meat with salt and pepper and shape into 6 flat patties. Coat meat patties with flour. Heat butter in frying-pan. Brown patties in butter and cook about 3 to 4 minutes on each side. The meat should be crisp and brown on the outside and pink inside. Transfer patties to hot serving dish and keep hot. Sauté onions in pan juices until golden brown. Drain on paper towelling. Place some onion on each patty and top with a fried egg. Serve with boiled potatoes.

Beef Stew with Bacon and Asparagus
Beef Sauté med Asparges

A welcome variation of a familiar dish.

½ lb. lean bacon
2 lb. stewing beef, cut into 1-in. cubes
½ oz. flour
1 teaspoon salt
1 large onion, chopped
8 fl. oz. beef bouillon
1 cup canned tomatoes or canned tomato sauce
4 peppercorns
4 whole cloves
⅓ cup chopped parsley
4 fl. oz. madeira or sherry (optional)
1 10-oz. package frozen asparagus spears

Place bacon in cold frying-pan and sauté slowly until crisp. Drain on paper towelling and reserve. Brown meat on all sides in bacon fat over high heat. Transfer meat to Dutch oven or heavy saucepan. Sprinkle with flour and salt. Add onion, beef bouillon, canned tomatoes, peppercorns, cloves, and parsley. Simmer, covered, over low heat about 2 to 3 hours, or until very tender. During last hour of cooking, add madeira or sherry. If no wine is used, add 4 fl. oz. hot bouillon. During last 10 minutes of cooking time, add frozen asparagus. At serving time, top with crisp bacon. Serve with mashed potatoes and pickled cucumbers.

NOTE: *Instead of frozen asparagus spears, canned white or green asparagus may be used. Add canned asparagus during last 3 minutes of cooking time.*

Simple Beef Stew · *Bankekød*

A surprisingly easy way of making a tasty family dish.

2 lb. lean stewing beef, in one piece
1½ oz. flour
1½ teaspoons salt
½ teaspoon pepper
3 oz. butter
2 bay leaves
Boiling water

Trim beef of all fat and cut into ½-inch slices. Pound them thin with a mallet. Cut meat into 1½-inch squares. Combine flour, salt, and pepper. Coat beef slices with flour mixture. Heat butter in Dutch oven or heavy saucepan. Brown meat slices in it on all sides. Add bay leaves and just enough boiling water to cover the meat. Simmer, covered, over low heat until meat is tender. (Cooking time depends on the cut of beef.) Stir occasionally. Check gravy for consistency; if necessary, thicken with a little more flour dissolved in a little cold water. Serve with mashed potatoes. Danish-style mashed potatoes are thinner than English, since about twice as much milk is added.

Parsley Hearts · *Stegte Hjerter*

Another old-fashioned and good Danish dish very well worth trying, especially when the wolf is at the door. A 4- to 5-lb. heart will serve 6; veal and pigs' hearts vary in size. Hearts are on the dry side and should be cooked slowly.

4 to 5 lb. hearts
6 oz. butter
2 cups chopped parsley
2 oz. flour
½ teaspoon salt
Water or beef bouillon
3 dessertspoons flour
2 fl. oz. cream
4 fl. oz. currant juice or jelly or cranberry juice cocktail

Cut hearts in half lengthwise. Carefully remove fat, arteries, veins, blood, and sinews. Wash thoroughly and dry. Cream half the butter. Work in parsley. Stuff hearts with parsley mixture. Sew hearts together. Roll in flour. Melt the remaining butter. Brown hearts on all sides in hot butter. Add salt and enough water or bouillon to cover the half hearts. Simmer, covered, for 3 hours, turning occasionally. Remove hearts when tender. Remove thread. Cut into medium-sized slices and keep hot. Add or remove enough water to make 2 cups. Stir in 3 dessertspoons flour blended with cream until smooth. Cook over low heat, stirring constantly, until thick and smooth. Stir in currant juice or jelly or cranberry juice cocktail. Reheat. Serve sauce over heart slices. Serve with sugar-browned potatoes* and vegetables or pickled beets* or pickled cucumbers.*

NOTE: *The hearts may also be stuffed with a mixture of peeled and cored apples and/or chopped prunes. A 4- to 5-lb. beef heart will take about 3 cups of stuffing. Since the hearts are dry, add 3 oz. butter to 3 cups of fruit stuffing.*

Tongue · *Oksetunge*

Tongue, either fresh, salted, or smoked, is a popular Danish dish. It is braised, boiled, baked, or used in aspics for smørrebrød. The recipes, however, resemble English ones, found in any standard cookbook.

Kirsten Christiansen's Potted Liver *Lever-gryde*

2 large carrots, thinly sliced
3 medium-sized onions, sliced
¼ lb. salt pork or Danish bacon, cubed
1¼ lb. liver, cut into ½-in. slices
Flour
2 oz. butter
Salt
Pepper
8 fl. oz. double cream
½ cup chopped parsley

Cook carrots and onions with salt pork or bacon until tender, stirring occasionally. Do not brown. Dredge liver with flour. Heat butter and cook liver in it until browned on all sides, or about 5 minutes. Add salt and pepper to taste. Combine vegetables and liver in one casserole, including the pan juices. Simmer, covered, over low heat about 10 minutes. Add cream and bring gently to the boil. Sprinkle with parsley and serve in casserole, with boiled potatoes on the side.

Danish Hash · *Hachis*

Any meat left-overs may be used for this dish. However, it is thoroughly worth while to make *hachis* with either the imported Danish luncheon meat or pork loin, or to use odds and ends of Danish ham.

3 cups left-over cooked meat, minced fine
2 medium-sized onions, finely chopped
2 oz. butter
1 oz. flour
12 fl. oz. beef bouillon
4 fl. oz. red wine (optional)
1 teaspoon gravy colouring
¼ cup chopped mixed pickles
½ teaspoon salt
6 fried eggs

Combine meat and onions. Heat butter in frying-pan and cook meat mixture in it until golden brown. Stir in flour.

Gradually stir in beef bouillon and red wine. Cook over low heat, stirring constantly, until smooth and thick. Stir in gravy colouring, pickles, and salt. Heat through thoroughly. Serve hot topped with fried eggs and sugar-browned potatoes.*

Danish Delight · *Biksemad*

I think this is the best way to use meat left-overs, especially when they include ham or Danish bacon.

3 cups left-over cooked meat
2 oz. butter
2 large onions, sliced
3 large potatoes, cooked, peeled, and diced
1 teaspoon salt
¼ teaspoon pepper
6 fried eggs

Cut meat into ½-inch cubes. Melt butter in a large frying-pan and brown meat. Remove meat and keep hot. Add onions to frying-pan. Cook over medium heat until tender. Add potatoes and cook until golden brown. Add meat and cook, stirring constantly, about 3 to 5 minutes, or until thoroughly heated through. Sprinkle with salt and pepper. Place a fried egg on each serving and serve with Worcestershire or any standard tomato or mushroom sauce.

NOTE: *The far-better-than-average taste of this hash is due to the fact that the ingredients are first cooked separately and then combined.*

Curried Oxtail · *Oksehale i Karry*

1 big or 2 small oxtails
2 oz. butter or margarine
1 large onion, chopped
1 dessertspoon curry powder
2 bay leaves
Water or bouillon
Salt
Pepper
Flour
8 fl. oz. double cream
15 small white onions, cooked
¼ cup chopped pimento

Cut oxtail into pieces at the joints. Heat butter in deep frying pan or casserole. Cook onion in it until golden. Stir in curry powder and cook 3 minutes, stirring constantly. Add oxtail pieces and brown on all sides. Add bay leaves, water or bouillon to cover, and salt and pepper to taste. Simmer, covered, over a low flame about 2½ to 3 hours, or until oxtail is tender. Thicken gravy with a little flour and add cream. Add onions and heat through. Garnish with pimento. Serve with rice or boiled potatoes.

Forcemeat Balls · *Kødboller*

These are served in soups, but they make an excellent light entrée with a standard mushroom sauce and a salad. The meat must be ground to a paste – this is best done in a blender – for perfect results.

¾ lb. raw boneless beef (any cut)
2 oz. beef suet
1 medium-sized onion
½ oz. flour
2 eggs, well beaten
½ teaspoon salt
½ teaspoon pepper
16 fl. oz. double cream, chilled

Run meat, suet, and onion through the electric blender, or mince together 5 times. Beat in flour, eggs, salt and pepper, beating well after each addition. Place mixture in a large bowl set in a bowl of ice and with a wooden spoon work to a smooth paste. Beat in the cream, a tablespoon at a time. The consistency should be that of firm whipped cream. Chill for about 1 hour. Thoroughly butter on all sides a deep frying-pan or a shallow saucepan. Shape forcemeat balls with two teaspoons dipped in water, by scooping out meat mixture with one spoon, smoothing out the top with the other spoon, and sliding the forcemeat ball into the buttered pan. Place the forcemeat balls in neat rows, allowing for expansion. To poach, pour almost but not quite boiling salted water *very gently* into the pan from the side, not disturbing the balls. The water should come about half-way up the forcemeat balls. Simmer gently for 5 to 8 minutes, depending on size. Remove with slotted spoon and place in hot soup or on hot serving-dish.

NOTE: *Before cooking all the forcemeat balls, cook one or two to see how they hold together. If not firm enough, beat in a little more flour,* 1 *teaspoon at a time. The secret is to have the mixture very cold, and to poach in water that barely quivers.*

Margrethe Schanne's Hamburger

Margrethe Schanne is a prima ballerina of the famous and superlative Danish Royal Ballet, and one of the great interpreters of romantic roles in such ballets as *Les Sylphides* and *Giselle*. She is also an excellent cook and housekeeper, which surprises one in so ethereal a creature.

4 small or medium-sized onions, thinly sliced
3 oz. butter
1 teaspoon sugar
1 lb. minced steak, shaped into 4 patties
Pepper
6 dessertspoons cognac
2 oz. butter, cut into pieces
Salt

Cook onions in 3 oz. butter and sugar until golden brown. Keep hot. Coat meat patties on one side with freshly ground black pepper to taste. Heat heavy frying-pan. Brown meat patties over high heat on both sides. Lower flame and add 4 dessertspoons cognac. Flame. When flames have died down, add 2 oz. butter. When butter is melted, add remaining cognac and flame. When flame has died down, salt meat patties. Serve on hot plates, with onions piled on top of each patty. Serve sauce separately or pour over meat. Serve with boiled new potatoes and a chicory salad dressed with salad dressing flavoured with a little garlic. Makes 4 servings.

NOTE: *This is an excellent hamburger variation. The trick is to cook the whole dish very quickly.*

Veal

Rosalie Holmes's Easter Veal

2 lb. boneless leg of veal
2 pints veal stock or chicken bouillon
5 medium-sized carrots, cut in pieces
15 very small white onions, peeled
5 sprigs parsley
1 stalk celery
1 bay leaf
¼ teaspoon thyme
4 peppercorns
1½ teaspoons salt
2 oz. butter
1 oz. flour
2 egg yolks
2 dessertspoons lemon juice
½ lb. small mushrooms, sautéed in a little butter

Have butcher tie meat to retain shape. Boil meat in water to cover over medium heat for 5 minutes. Drain; remove scum. Place veal in deep saucepan and add veal stock or chicken bouillon, carrots, and onions. Tie parsley, celery, bay leaf, thyme, and peppercorns in small piece of cheesecloth and add to meat. Add salt. Bring mixture to the boil and skim, if necessary. Lower heat and simmer, covered, about 1¼ hours or until veal is tender. Remove meat, carrots, and onions and keep hot. Strain broth and keep hot. Heat butter and stir in flour. Gradually add hot broth and cook over low heat, stirring constantly, until sauce is thick and smooth. Beat egg yolks with lemon juice. Remove sauce from heat and stir in egg mixture. Add hot mushrooms to sauce. Heat through thoroughly without boiling. Slice veal. Place on hot platter and surround with carrots and onions. Pour sauce over meat. Serve with rice or mashed potatoes.

Kirsten Christiansen's Modern Fricandeau

1½ lb. boneless veal, shoulder or leg
4–5 oz. flour for cooking
3 oz. butter
8 fl. oz. water
8 fl. oz. milk
¼ lb. mushrooms, sliced
1 oz. butter
½ oz. flour
8 fl. oz. double cream
Salt
Pepper
8 slices bacon, cooked and drained

Cut veal into 1½-inch cubes; coat with flour. Heat 2 oz. butter in deep frying-pan or casserole and brown meat in it on all sides. Add water and milk. Simmer, covered, until tender. Cook mushrooms in butter until soft but still firm. Stir flour into cream to make a smooth paste. Stir into mushrooms and cook about 3 minutes, stirring constantly. Pour mushroom sauce over veal and top with bacon slices.

Mock Chicken · *Forloren Kylling*

6 thin slices of boneless veal (about 1¼ lb.)
½ teaspoon salt
¼ teaspoon pepper
5 oz. butter
6 dessertspoons chopped parsley
2 oz. flour
8 fl. oz. single or double cream
1 teaspoon gravy colouring

Pound veal slices very thin. Keep meat in one piece and avoid making holes. Sprinkle with salt and pepper. Cream 3 oz. butter and work in parsley. Place 2 dessertspoons of the butter mixture in the centre of each slice of meat. Roll meat around butter. Tie with string. Coat veal rolls with flour. Heat 2 oz. butter in a frying-pan for 45 minutes. Add cream and gravy colouring and simmer, uncovered, until cream is half absorbed. Remove string and place rolls on hot platter. Cover with sauce. Serve with vegetables and boiled potatoes arranged in alternate mounds around the veal rolls. Makes 4 servings.

Wiener Schnitzel

Though this is not of Danish origin, it can be counted as a Danish dish because of the popularity it enjoys with all Danes.

6 boneless veal cutlets
4 oz. butter
6 lemon slices
6 rolled anchovies
Capers
2 to 3 dessertspoons cream

Sauté veal cutlets in hot butter for 2 minutes on either side. Turn again and cook until done, about 10 to 15 minutes, depending on the thickness of the veal cutlets. Place on hot serving-dish and top with lemon slices. Place a rolled anchovy on each lemon slice and top with capers. Stir cream into pan juices, heat through, and pour over veal cutlets, avoiding the garnish of lemon, anchovies, and capers.

Veal Tournedos · *Kalvetournedos*

6 veal rosettes or ***noisettes de veau*****, about 1 in. thick**
2 oz. butter
1 medium-sized onion, chopped
½ lb. sliced mushrooms
6 fl. oz. dry red wine
6 fl. oz. bouillon
1 dessertspoon tomato purée
Flour
Salt
Pepper
Cooked marrow

Cook veal in hot butter in heavy frying-pan until browned on all sides. Transfer to hot plate; keep hot. Cook onion and mushrooms in frying-pan juices until onion is soft. Add wine and bouillon. Stir in tomato purée. Return veal rosettes to frying-pan. Simmer, covered, over low heat until meat is tender. Transfer to hot serving-dish and keep hot. Thicken sauce with a little flour mixed with water to desired consistency. Season with salt and pepper to taste. Pour sauce over veal. Top each rosette with a thick piece of cooked marrow. Place buttered green peas at one end of serving dish and browned potatoes at the other. In between, place grilled tomato halves or slices. Decorate with parsley sprigs.

NOTE: *Thick boneless veal cutlets may be prepared in the same manner.*

Sailor's Stew · *Skipperlabskovs*

A fine, stick-to-the-ribs casserole, whose flavour is vastly improved by the use of beer.

5 oz. butter
1½ lb. boneless beef or veal cut in 1-in. cubes
3 onions, chopped
24 fl. oz. beer or ale
24 fl. oz. beef bouillon
1 teaspoon salt
12 peppercorns
2 bay leaves
6 medium-sized potatoes, peeled and cut into ½-in. cubes
3 dessertspoons chopped chives or green onion tops

Melt 2 oz. butter in large pan. Add meat and onions. Cook, stirring frequently, until onions are transparent but not brown. Add beer, bouillon, salt, peppercorns, and bay leaves. Make sure that you have sufficient liquid to cover meat; if necessary, add more beer or bouillon or water. Simmer, covered, over low heat for 20 minutes. Add potatoes. Continue simmering, covered, until meat is tender and potatoes have fallen apart and thickened the broth – about 1½ to 2 hours. Cut the remaining 3 oz. butter into 6 pats or shape into 6 small balls. Serve butter in each serving of sailor's stew and sprinkle with chives.

Danish Meat Balls · *Frikadeller*

There are as many ways of making *frikadeller* as there are cooks in Denmark, since this is *the* most popular of all meat dishes. *Frikadeller* are eaten hot or cold. They should be light, and one of the secrets of lightness is to use soda water in the mixture. They can be made entirely of one kind of meat if desired.

½ lb. boneless raw veal or beef
½ lb. boneless raw pork
1 medium-sized onion
3 tablespoons flour or sifted breadcrumbs
A good ½ pint soda water or milk
1 egg, well beaten
1 teaspoon salt
½ teaspoon pepper
3 oz. butter

Run meats and onion twice through the electric meat grinder or 4 times through the finest blade of a hand mincer. Stir in flour or bread crumbs; beat thoroughly. Gradually beat in soda water or milk, 2 tablespoons at a time, beating constantly to aerate mixture. Beat in egg, salt, and pepper. Beat mixture until puffy. Shape mixture into oblongs with two teaspoons dipped in water. Fry *frikadeller* in hot butter slowly until browned on all sides. Serve with boiled or sugar-browned potatoes* and red cabbage* or pickled beets,* or use on the cold table.

NOTE: *Frikadeller made with milk and bread crumbs are not as light but they are easier to handle.*

Meat Balls in Celery Sauce
Kødboller med Sellerisauce

1 or 2 celeriacs (about 1½ lb.) or 3 cups sliced celery
1 recipe forcemeat (see stuffed cabbage)*
2 oz. butter
1 oz. flour
24 fl. oz. water or vegetable broth
1 teaspoon salt
¼ teaspoon pepper
2 egg yolks (optional)

Peel and dice celery root. Prepare forcemeat as in recipe for stuffed cabbage. Shape mixture into small balls and drop into gently boiling water. Simmer over low heat for 5 minutes or until firm. Remove with a slotted spoon and place into hot serving-dish. Keep hot. Add celery root or celery slices to water in which the meat was cooked. Simmer for about 15 minutes, or until tender. Drain and reserve vegetable broth. Add celery to meat balls. Measure 24 fl. oz. vegetable broth. Melt butter and stir in flour. Gradually stir in vegetable broth, salt, and pepper. Cook over low heat until smooth and thick. Remove heat and beat egg yolks into sauce. Blend thoroughly. Pour hot sauce over meat balls and celery. Decorate with triangles of puff-pastry or rich piecrust.

Kidney Stew with Cocktail Sausages and Scrambled Eggs

Nyreragout med Karbonadepølser og Røraeg

A good combination of flavours.

2 veal kidneys
Salt
Pepper
1 oz. butter or margarine
1 large onion, chopped
Water or bouillon
2 bay leaves
2 dessertspoons tomato purée
Flour
16 cocktail sausages
3 eggs
3 dessertspoons milk or cream
1½ oz. butter

Trim veal kidneys of fat and membranes and cut into ¼-inch slices. Sprinkle with salt and pepper. Heat 1 oz. butter in deep frying-pan or casserole. Sauté kidney slices and onion in it about 3 minutes. Add water or bouillon to cover, bay leaves, and tomato purée. Simmer, covered, over low heat until tender. Thicken gravy to desired consistency with a little flour. Heat cocktail sausages and scramble eggs beaten with milk or cream in 1½ oz. butter while kidneys are cooking. Top casserole with sausages and scrambled eggs. Serve with french bread or mashed potatoes.

Braised Calf's Heart · *Kalvehjerter*

Very popular in Denmark and surprisingly good.

3 veal hearts
1 cup chopped parsley
1 cup chopped cooked stoned prunes
½ cup chopped onion
1 oz. butter or margarine
2 carrots, sliced
1 stalk celery, sliced
1 bay leaf
5 whole peppercorns
1 teaspoon salt
About 1 pint water or more
4 fl. oz. double cream

With a sharp knife remove fat, arteries, veins, and blood from hearts. Wash and dry carefully. Combine parsley, prunes, and onion. Stuff heart cavities with mixture. Close opening with skewers or toothpicks and tie with string to retain shape. Melt butter or margarine in heavy saucepan. Brown hearts in it on all sides. Add all other ingredients except cream. Cover tightly and simmer over lowest possible heat about 2 hours, or until hearts are tender. Stir occasionally and, if necessary, add a little more water, a tablespoon at a time. When the hearts are cooked there should be about ⅓ pint pan liquid. Stir in the cream and do not boil again. Serve with boiled or mashed potatoes and a green vegetable or salad.

NOTE: *This dish can also be made with a beef heart, but then it must be cooked longer. A* 4- *to* 5-*lb. beef heart will serve* 6, *a veal heart* 1 *or* 2.

Mock Turtle · *Forloren Skildapadde*

This is a classic of old-fashioned Danish cooking, and no Danish cookbook should be without it. To my readers who may come across a calf's head, I can only cry: '*En avant*! The path is arduous, but the results very flavourful indeed.'

1 calf's head
2 tablespoons salt
1 recipe minced fish (*fiskefars*)*
1 recipe Danish meat balls (*frikadeller*)*
1½ oz. butter
3 dessertspoons flour
4 fl. oz. madeira
1 calf's brain
10 oz. firm white bread (about 10 slices)

4 oz. butter
4 onions, sliced
4 carrots, sliced
2 leeks, chopped
1 celeriac, peeled and cubed, or 1 cup sliced celery
3 dessertspoons tomato paste
2 teaspoons gravy colouring
2 beef bouillon cubes
8 fl. oz. milk
1 oz. butter
1½ dessertspoons flour
2 egg yolks
1 teaspoon salt
¼ teaspoon pepper
2 egg whites, stiffly beaten
Deep fat or boiling water
6 hard-boiled eggs

Split calf's head. Remove tongue, brain, and eyes. Cover tongue with water. Bring, tightly covered, to the boil and simmer until tender. Drain and cool. Skin tongue and cut into 1-inch squares. Soak head for 2 hours in cold water. Clean head and scald with boiling water. Cover head with salt and water. Bring, tightly covered, to the boil and simmer for 2 to 3 hours, or until meat loosens from the bones. Drain head and reserve stock. Cool head. Remove meat from bones. Place meat in a bowl. Cover and place a heavy weight on top. Chill overnight. Remove weight and cut meat into 1-inch squares.

Prepare minced fish.*

Prepare Danish meat balls.*

In deep pan, melt 4 oz. butter and brown. Add onions, carrots, leeks, celeriac or celery, tomato paste, gravy colouring, bouillon cubes, and stock from calf's head. Simmer, covered, for 1½ hours. Strain. Melt 1½ oz. butter. Stir in 3 dessertspoons flour. Gradually stir in strained stock. Cook over low heat, stirring constantly, until smooth and thickened. Stir in madeira.

Add calf's-head meat, tongue, meat balls, and minced fish balls to the sauce. Keep hot. Prepare brain balls. These must be made at the last moment as they are fragile. Soak brain in salted water for 2 hours. Remove outer membrane. Strain through a sieve. Trim crusts off bread. Break bread into pieces. Add milk. Soak for 15 minutes. Melt 1 oz. butter and stir in 1½ dessertspoons flour. Add soaked bread, with excess milk squeezed out. Stir over low heat until mixture thickens and pulls from the sides of the pan. Remove from heat. Beat in sieved brain. Beat in egg yolks, salt, and pepper.

Fold in egg whites. Drop by teaspoonfuls into deep fat heated to 380° F. and cook for 2 to 3 minutes. Or drop into barley simmering water and cook until balls rise to the surface. Drain and add to sauce. Place half a hard-boiled egg for each serving into the mock turtle. Makes about 12 servings.

NOTE: *Most Danes buy this dish tinned.*

Stuffed Cabbage · *Farseret Kaal*

A very good family dish.

Forcemeat

1 lb. boneless veal or ½ lb. boneless veal and ½ lb. boneless pork
½ teaspoon salt
1 egg, well beaten
16 fl. oz. cold milk or single cream
⅔ cup flour
½ teaspoon salt
½ teaspoon pepper
1 medium-sized onion, grated
1 large white cabbage (about 3 to 4 lb.)

Run the meat through the finest blade of the mincer 5 times or blend in electric blender. Beat in ½ teaspoon salt, egg, and flour. Blend thoroughly. Gradually beat in milk or cream, about 2 tablespoons at a time. Beat in ½ teaspoon salt, pepper, and grated onion. Trim outside leaves of cabbage. Cut off a lid at the stalk end of the cabbage. Hollow out the cabbage with a sharp knife, leaving a shell about ¾ inch thick. Spoon forcemeat into cabbage. Replace lid on cabbage. Tie cabbage into several layers of muslin. Place into gently boiling hot water to cover. Simmer, covered, over low heat for about 2 hours. Carefully remove cabbage from muslin. Cut into wedges and serve with melted butter.

NOTE: *Shape remaining meat mixture, if any, into small balls, and simmer 5 minutes in barely simmering water. Remove and use in soup.*

Stuffed Cauliflower · *Farseret Blomkaal*

A good luncheon or supper dish with an interesting flavour combination.

1 large cauliflower
Salt
Boiling water
Flour
1½ recipes Danish meat balls (*frikadeller*)*
2 hard-boiled egg yolks, chopped

Trim cauliflower. Cover with boiling salted water and cook for 5 minutes. Drain; reserve liquid. Place several layers of thin muslin over the head of the cauliflower. Mark the area of cloth which completely covers the cauliflower. Remove cloth and spread it out. Sprinkle cloth with flour. Spread the Danish meat ball mixture over marked area of cloth. Place cauliflower stem downwards on the meat. Tie cloth around cauliflower, to form a ball. Bring reserved cauliflower liquid to the boil. Place cauliflower ball in liquid, adding sufficient boiling water to cover. Simmer over low heat for 20 minutes, or until cauliflower tests tender. Remove from liquid and cool 2 to 3 minutes. Remove cloth carefully. Place on hot platter and garnish with chopped hard-boiled egg yolks. Cut into wedges. Serve with tomato sauce or melted butter.

Lamb

Lamb with Dill · *Lam i Dild*

3 lb. breast of lamb
Salt
Pepper
1 large carrot, sliced
1 medium-sized onion, diced
$\frac{1}{2}$ cup diced celery
$\frac{1}{4}$–$\frac{1}{2}$ oz. flour, depending on how thick a sauce is wanted
Water
1 dessertspoon vinegar
1 teaspoon sugar
4 fl. oz. double cream
2 egg yolks
Chopped dill (about $\frac{3}{4}$ cup or more)

Trim meat of excess fat and cut into 2-inch cubes. Sprinkle with salt and pepper. Place in deep pan. Add carrot, onion, celery, and water to cover. Simmer, covered, over low heat about 1 to 1$\frac{1}{4}$ hours, or until meat is tender. Skim as needed and stir occasionally. Drain liquid into a saucepan and cook down to about $\frac{1}{2}$ pint. Mix flour with a little water and stir into liquid. Cook until smooth and thickened, stirring constantly. Stir in vinegar and sugar. Beat together cream and egg yolks. Stir into sauce. Pour sauce over meat and heat through thoroughly. Sprinkle with chopped dill before serving. Serve with boiled potatoes and cucumber salad.

Whitsuntide Lamb · *Pinselam*

It is impossible to specify the exact amounts of water and bouillon since they depend on the size of the cooking pot used. By the same token, the amount of flour needed to thicken the sauce has to be adjusted to the liquid.

2 lb. breast of lamb
Water or bouillon
3 medium-sized carrots, chopped
1 cup chopped celery
¼ cup chopped parsley
Salt
Pepper
1 10-oz. package frozen peas
Flour
2 egg yolks
½ cup chopped parsley

Trim lamb of excess fat and cut into cubes. Place in deep pan and add water or bouillon to cover, carrots, celery, parsley, and salt and pepper to taste. Simmer, covered, over low heat until meat is just tender, skimming as needed. Add frozen peas and cook until tender. Thicken pan liquid with flour and stir in egg yolks. Sprinkle with plenty of chopped parsley. Serve with boiled parsleyed potatoes.

Pickled Lamb · *Spraengt Lam*

Pickling meat is an historic way of preserving it. This lamb dish is worth the attention of modern cooks, provided that the lamb, like Danish lamb, is really young and tender. Athletic, adolescent lamb won't do.

6 lb. breast or shoulder of spring lamb
2 oz. salt
¾ teaspoon saltpetre
2 oz. brown or white sugar

Wash meat and trim off excess fat. Mix salt with saltpetre and sugar. Rub meat thoroughly on all sides with salt mixture. Place meat in a deep bowl. Do not use aluminium. Let stand, covered, for 3 to 4 days, in refrigerator or in a cool place. Turn meat every day and rub with the brine that forms around the meat. Remove the meat. Wash under running cold water. Place meat in deep pan and cover with water. Simmer, covered, over low heat 2 to 3 hours or until meat is tender. Cut meat into individual servings and place on hot serving-platter. Surround with buttered vegetables and serve with boiled potatoes and melted butter.

Lamb Chops with Danish Blue Cheese

4 oz. Danish Blue cheese
2 dessertspoons double cream
6 lamb chops

Combine Danish Blue cheese and cream; blend to a smooth paste. Grill lamb chops in the usual manner. Just before they are done, spread each chop with cheese and continue grilling until cheese is bubbly. Serve with a salad of watercress and chicory.

Grilled Lamb's Head · *Grilleret Lammehoved*

The old-fashioned Danish housewife didn't waste a thing. Personally, I prefer to cook and eat more impersonal food. One lamb's head will serve 2.

3 lambs' heads
6 oz. fine dry bread crumbs
2 teaspoons salt
1 teaspoon pepper
2 dessertspoons chopped parsley
3 eggs, well beaten
4 oz. butter

Ask the butcher to split each head in half. Remove brains and tongues. Clean heads. Soak in cold water for 2 hours. Drain. In deep pan, place heads and tongues in boiling salt water to cover. Cook heads and tongues until the skin can be removed easily – about 1 to 2 hours. Trim and clean the heads. Remove roof of mouth, eyes, and ears. (A Danish cookbook begs the cook not to remove the fat behind the eyes, since experts claim that this is the best part of the whole head.) Cut tongues in halves. Mix breadcrumbs with salt, pepper, and parsley. Dip tongue and head into beaten eggs and coat with bread-crumbs. Heat butter in frying-pan. Brown heads and tongues on all sides until golden brown. Serve with spinach, cauliflower, asparagus, or other vegetables.

Pork

Marinated Roast Pork · *Marineret Stegt Svinekam*

This is a very Danish and excellent way of preparing pork. The recipe comes from the Rødvig Kro, an inn by the Baltic Sea.

1- to 5-lb. loin of pork or any other pork roast
2 large onions, sliced
2 carrots, sliced
2 stalks celery, sliced
5 bay leaves
8 whole peppercorns
Dry red wine
3 oz. butter
Salt

Trim excess fat off meat. Place in deep bowl. Do not use aluminium. Top meat with onions, carrots, celery, bay leaves, and peppercorns. Add enough red wine to cover. Store in cool place or refrigerate for at least 24 hours. Drain pork and wipe dry. Strain marinade and reserve. Melt butter in a large pan. Brown pork in it on all sides. Pour off butter. Add about 8 fl. oz. of the marinade and salt to taste. Cover very tightly and simmer over low heat about 30 to 40 minutes to the pound, or until meat thermometer registers 185° F. Check for moisture during cooking time; if necessary, add more marinade as needed. Remove to hot serving-platter and slice. Make cream gravy with pan drippings in the usual manner and add sautéed sliced mushrooms to it.

Or else transfer the pork browned in butter to rack in baking-pan. Bake in 350° F., gas mark 4, oven 30 to 40 minutes to the pound, basting frequently with marinade. Use pan drippings for cream gravy.

Fillet of Pork with Apples and Prunes

Mørbrad med Aebler og Svesker

A favourite of Chef Karl Holst of the Copenhagen Restaurant in New York.

2 fresh pork fillets, about 1½ lb. each
2 tart apples, peeled and cored
1 cup prunes
3 oz. butter
Water
½ oz. flour
2 fl. oz. water, milk, or cream (for a richer gravy)

Trim fillets of excess fat and remove sinews. Cut in half lengthwise, forming a long pocket. Mince apples. Cover prunes with boiling water for 5 minutes. Drain; remove stones and chop coarsely. Combine apples and prunes. Stuff filling into pocket of meat. Tie with a white string or skewer opening. Melt butter in a large pan. Brown meat on all sides. Add barely enough water to cover meat. Simmer, covered, for about 35 to 40 minutes to the pound. Remove meat and keep hot. Combine flour and water or milk or cream and stir to a smooth paste. Add to hot meat stock. Cook over low heat, stirring constantly, until gravy is smooth and thickened. Cut meat into slices and place on hot platter. Cover with gravy and serve with boiled potatoes and any vegetables.

Roast Pork with Crackling · *Flaeskesteg med Svaer*

1 fresh ham or shoulder with the rind on (about 3 lb. for every 6 servings)
2 dessertspoons salt
8 fl. oz. water
2 teaspoons beef extract or bottled gravy essence
2 dessertspoons flour

Score the rind of the meat with a sharp knife lengthwise and crosswise, spacing cuts ½ inch apart. Wash meat in cold water and dry. Rub thoroughly with salt on all sides. Preheat oven to 350° F., gas mark 4. Place roast on a rack in a shallow roasting-pan and roast for 15 minutes. Pour the water into the roasting-pan. Do not baste roast, or rind won't be crisp. Roast about 30 minutes to the pound, or until meat thermometer registers internal temperature of 185° F. Remove meat and keep hot. Pour dripping from roasting-pan. Add enough water to make about 16 fl. oz. Add beef extract or gravy essence. Blend flour with a little water. Stir until smooth. Add to pan dripping. Stir over low heat until smooth and thick. Or substitute cream for water for a richer gravy. Slice meat. Arrange meat slices at one end of oblong serving-platter. Pile a mound of Danish-style red cabbage* at the other. Arrange sugar-browned potatoes* and small boiled potatoes on sides of platter. Decorate with lettuce leaves. Serve gravy separately.

Pork Fillet with Horse-radish

Svinemørbrad med Peberrod

2 to 3 pork fillets
Salt
Pepper
About 2–3 oz. butter, depending on size of meat
1 medium-sized onion, chopped
6 fl. oz. white vinegar
16 fl. oz. water or bouillon
1 dessertspoon flour
2–3 fl. oz. double cream
Fresh grated horse-radish

Cut fillets crosswise into ¾-inch slices. Sprinkle with salt and pepper. Heat butter in deep, heavy frying-pan. Cook meat slices and onion in it until browned on all sides. Add vinegar and water or bouillon. Simmer, covered, over low heat about 35 to 40 minutes, or until tender. Remove fillet slices and place on hot serving dish. Keep hot. Reduce frying-pan liquid to about ¾ pint. Blend flour with heavy cream to a smooth paste. Stir mixture slowly into frying-pan. Cook about 3 to 5 minutes to desired consistency. Pour sauce over meat slices. Sprinkle fresh grated horse-radish to taste over sauce. Serve with boiled potatoes.

Pork Fillet with Red Wine · *Mørbrad i Rødvin*

1 1½-to 2-lb. pork fillet
1 oz. butter
2 medium-sized onions, chopped
1 teaspoon salt
½ teaspoon pepper
8–10 fl. oz. dry red wine
½ lb. mushrooms, sliced
½ oz. butter
½ oz. flour
8 fl. oz. double cream

Cut fillet into 6 to 8 slices. Heat 1 oz. butter in frying-pan. Brown meat slices in it over high heat about 1 to 2 minutes on each side. Transfer to casserole. Brown onions in frying-pan juices. Top meat slices with onion. Sprinkle with salt and pepper and add wine. Cover and bake in 350° F., gas mark 4, oven about 1 to 1½ hours, or until meat is tender. While meat is cooking, sauté mushrooms in butter for about 3 minutes. Add to casserole 15 minutes before meat is tender. When meat is ready, stir flour into cream to make a smooth paste. Place meat on hot serving-dish and keep hot. Stir in cream mixture. Cook over lowest possible heat about 3 minutes, but do not let boil. Pour sauce over meat. Serve with home-fried potatoes and a green vegetable, and a side dish of apple sauce mixed with horse-radish to taste.

NOTE: *In Denmark, cooked crisp bacon is placed on top of the meat. I think this is too much of a good thing.*

Pork and Cabbage · *Flaesk i Kaal*

Another one of those simple Danish country dishes that rely on first-class ingredients for their success. Try it with either imported Danish bacon or home-cured bacon.

2 lb. lean salt pork or bacon, in one piece
1 large head of white cabbage (about 2 to 3 lb.)
6 peppercorns
1 bay leaf

Place salt pork or bacon in deep pan and cover with water. Bring to the boil and simmer 30 minutes. Drain and reserve broth. Place meat on the bottom of a large pan. Cut cabbage into 6 wedges. Trim off tough stalk. Place cabbage over meat. Add a small amount of the reserved broth. Add peppercorns and bay leaf. Cook, covered, over low heat for 3 hours, or until bacon and cabbage are tender. Stir meat and cabbage occasionally, adding additional small amounts of broth to prevent sticking. When cooked, the cabbage should be golden brown. Slice bacon, place on hot platter, and surround with cabbage.

NOTE: *If preferred, the pork or bacon may be sliced before cooking.*

Spare-ribs and Brown Cabbage · *Flaesk i Brunkaal*

1 large head of white cabbage (about 2 to 3 lb.)
1½ oz. sugar
1½ oz. butter
4 fl. oz. water
3 lb. fresh or smoked pork spare-ribs

Remove outer leaves from cabbage and core. Shred coarsely. In large saucepan, brown sugar until the colour of caramel. Stir in butter. Cook over low heat, stirring constantly, about

5 minutes. Add shredded cabbage and brown well. Add water. Simmer, covered, over low heat about 1 hour. Stir occasionally. Cut spare-ribs into 6 serving pieces. Add to cabbage and cover. Cook for 1 hour or until cabbage and meat are tender. Stir occasionally. If necessary, add a little more water to prevent sticking.

Roast Spare-ribs with Apples and Prunes

Ribbenssteg

An excellent dish.

4 lb. lean spare-ribs in one piece
4 small tart apples, peeled, cored, and chopped
1 cup prunes, soaked, stoned, and chopped
1 teaspoon salt
½ teaspoon pepper

Have the butcher crack the spare-rib bones in half lengthwise. Trim free of excess fat. Combine chopped apples and prunes. Spread spare-ribs with a layer of fruit. Fold spare-ribs in half then skewer or toothpick the edges together. Sprinkle with salt and pepper. Place on rack in shallow baking-pan. Roast in 350° F., gas mark 4, oven for 1½ hours. Serve with red cabbage,* pickled beets,* and gravy made from dripping.

Small Frankfurters in White Wine Sauce

Små Karbonadepølser i Hvidvinssauce

1 lb. small (cocktail) frankfurters
1 oz. butter
½ oz. flour
8 fl. oz. dry white wine
8 fl. oz. double cream
Toasted white bread
⅓ cup chopped parsley
6 slices bacon, cooked

Prick frankfurters with a fork to prevent bursting during cooking. Heat butter in frying-pan and brown frankfurters in it. Sprinkle with flour. Stir in white wine and heat frankfurters thoroughly. Stir in cream. Heat, but do not boil. Spoon over toasted white bread, sprinkle with parsley, and garnish with bacon slices.

Marinated Pork · *Marineret Flaesk*

Good for a cold supper.

2 to 3 lb. loin of pork, boned
Water
2 bay leaves
1 large onion
1 teaspoon salt
½ teaspoon pepper
2 sprigs parsley or 2 tablespoons dried parsley

Marinade

16 fl. oz. wine or cider vinegar
5 peppercorns
1 large onion, sliced
2 bay leaves

Place meat in deep pan. Cover with water. Add bay leaves, onion, salt, pepper, and parsley. Simmer, covered, over low heat about 35 to 40 minutes to the pound, or until thoroughly cooked through. Remove meat from liquid, cool, and slice thinly. Combine all marinade ingredients and bring to the boil. Cool. Place meat in deep bowl (do not use aluminium) and pour marinade over it. Let stand for about 4 hours. Drain and serve with boiled potatoes, dark rye bread, mustard, and pickled beets.*

Cold Roast Veal or Pork Soubise

Kalve eller Svinekød Soubise

A Steensgaard recipe for left-overs.

Cold roast veal or pork, sliced
Butter
Creamed spinach

Cook cold meat slices in hot butter until golden. Place in buttered baking-dish. Cover with creamed spinach and top with soubise sauce. Place in hot oven or under grill until golden and bubbly.

Soubise or Onion Sauce

1½ oz. butter
3 dessertspoons flour
1¼ pints chicken or veal stock
Salt
Pepper
⅛ teaspoon nutmeg
3 large onions, minced
1½ oz. butter
3 dessertspoons double cream, whipped

Melt 1½ oz. butter in heavy saucepan and stir in flour. Gradually stir in chicken or veal stock, and cook, stirring constantly, until thickened and smooth. Season with salt and pepper to taste and nutmeg. Cook onions in 1½ oz. butter until soft and transparent. Do not brown. Add onions to sauce and simmer, covered, over low heat 30 minutes, stirring occasionally. Strain through a fine sieve or purée in blender. Taste for seasonings and add salt and pepper, if necessary. Fold in whipped cream. Makes about 1 pint of sauce.

Bacon with Parsley Sauce

Stegt Flaesk med Persillesauce

Made with flavourful bacon, such as tinned Danish bacon, this dish turns out to be simple but tasty.

1½ lb. thinly sliced lean bacon or lean salt pork

Sauce

2 oz. butter
½ oz. flour
8 fl. oz. milk or cream
¼ teaspoon salt
¼ teaspoon sugar
⅓ cup minced parsley

Fry bacon or salt pork until crisp. Drain. Serve hot with parsley sauce and boiled potatoes.

To make *sauce*, melt 1 oz. butter. Stir in flour. Gradually stir in milk or cream. Cook over low heat, stirring constantly, until smooth and thick. Stir in salt and sugar. Stir in parsley just before serving. Pour sauce into gravy-boat and top with the remaining butter. Serve hot over bacon.

Apples Stuffed with Bacon · *Aebler med Flaesk*

6 slices lean bacon, minced
1 small onion, minced
$\frac{1}{8}$ teaspoon sage
6 baking apples
About $\frac{1}{4}$ pint water
$\frac{1}{4}$ cup chopped parsley

Cook bacon, onion, and sage until soft and golden. Peel and core apples. Stuff cavities with bacon mixture. Place apples in well-greased baking-dish. Add water. Cover with lid or aluminium foil. Bake, covered, in 350° F., gas mark 4, oven until apples are tender. Baste once or twice with pan juices or a little additional water. Do not overcook; apples must retain their shape. Sprinkle with chopped parsley. Serve with any roast or fowl.

Pork and Apples 1 · *Aebleflaesk*

Good for breakfast or supper.

12 slices Danish bacon or pork loin or slightly salted pork
6 large tart apples, cored but not peeled
3 oz. sugar

Fry bacon or pork until crisp. Drain and keep hot. Cut apples into 8 wedges each. Sprinkle with sugar. Fry apples in hot bacon fat. Turn carefully and fry until soft but not mushy. Pour apples into hot serving dish. Arrange bacon or pork slices on top of them in overlapping rows.

Pork and Apples 2 · *Aebleflaesk*

This version is better suited for lunch or supper.

4 strips lean bacon
12 thinly sliced loin pork chops (about $1\frac{1}{2}$ lb.), boned
Salt
Pepper
6 medium-sized tart apples
1 to 2 oz. sugar

Fry bacon until crisp. Remove bacon. Salt and pepper loin chops and fry in hot bacon fat until browned on all sides. Lower heat and cook until meat is tender. Remove meat and keep hot. Core apples and cut each into 8 wedges. Cook apple in hot pan dripping until tender but still firm. Add just enough sugar to keep apples tart. Pour apples into serving-dish. Arrange pork chops around them or on top of them and sprinkle with crumbled bacon.

Ham

The flavour of a ham depends on what the pig was fed and how carefully it was cured. Danish pigs are fed on fresh buttermilk from the dairies, among other things, and all of their food is fresh and extremely clean. The curing, too, is strictly supervised to maintain a constant high quality. Danish ham, which is imported into this country, ranks among the finest, since it is lean and very flavourful.

Since all tinned hams are boneless, if they are to be served whole, they look better with a glaze or garnish.

Beer – good flavourful Danish beer like Carlsberg or Tuborg – is the best drink to serve with ham, since the flavourful meat is apt to overwhelm a fine wine. But if you want to serve wine with your ham, choose a young fruity one, such as a rosé.

Tinned Danish ham should be baked in a 300° to 325° F., gas mark 2–3, oven 7 to 10 minutes to the pound, and basted during baking time.

Basting Liquids. Peach, pineapple, and apricot juice give ham a pleasant flavour. So does the juice of pickled peaches, cider, and fresh orange juice. Sherry, madeira, and marsala give ham an even better taste.

Baked Ham · *Stegt Skinke*

1 6-lb. tinned Danish ham
French or other prepared mustard
16 fl. oz. madeira or sherry
Freshly ground pepper
Fine dry breadcrumbs

Drain tinned ham and place in roasting-pan. Add madeira or sherry. Bake, covered, in 325° F., gas mark 2–3, oven for about 1¼ hours. Cool in pan. Baste ham occasionally with pan juices while cooling. Spread top with mustard. Sprinkle with pepper and press breadcrumbs into ham.

Basting Sauce for Tinned Ham

8 fl. oz. cider or apple juice
½ lb. light or dark brown sugar
1 dessertspoon vinegar
10 cloves
½ teaspoon salt
⅛ teaspoon cayenne pepper
1 stick cinnamon

Combine all ingredients and simmer, covered, for 10 minutes, over low heat, stirring occasionally.

Quick Jellied Ham

1 3-oz. package lemon-flavoured gelatin
1 teaspoon salt
8 fl. oz. boiling water
8 fl. oz. cold water
2 dessertspoons vinegar
2 teaspoons minced onion
Dash Tabasco
2 dessertspoons prepared horse-radish
1 cup Danish ham, diced
3 dessertspoons chopped sweet pickles
¾ cup chopped cabbage
Lettuce
Watercress

Dissolve gelatin and salt in boiling water. Stir in cold water, vinegar, onion, Tabasco, and horse-radish. Chill until slightly thickened. Fold in ham, pickles, and cabbage. Pour into lightly oiled individual moulds or into 1½ pint mould. Chill until firm. Unmould on a bed of shredded lettuce and garnish with watercress. Serve with horse-radish sauce with fresh cream* or mayonnaise with horse-radish.*

NOTE: *Chopped tongue or chopped Danish canned pork loin may be used instead of the ham.*

Ham with Madeira Sauce · *Skinke med Madeira*

6 ½-in.-thick slices Danish ham
½ oz. butter
¼ oz. flour
2 teaspoons tomato paste
Freshly ground pepper
8 fl. oz. madeira
5 fl. oz. double cream
¼ cup chopped parsley

Trim ham slices to uniform size. Arrange in overlapping row in buttered shallow baking-dish. Melt butter and stir in flour and tomato paste. Add pepper to taste and gradually stir in madeira. Cook over low heat, stirring constantly, until mixture thickens. Remove from heat and stir in cream. Add parsley. Pour sauce over ham and bake in 375° F., gas mark 5–6, oven until ham is heated through – about 7 to 10 minutes. Serve with grilled mushroom caps and braised chicory.

Vegetables and Salads

Asparagus · *Asparges*

Asparagus, both fresh and tinned, is much prized in Denmark. Danish asparagus is snow white, and the stalks are thick. (This asparagus can be bought tinned or bottled.) Fresh white asparagus should be peeled from below the head, increasing the thickness of the peel as the base is approached to remove any bitter flavour. It is then tied in bundles with white string, steamed standing upright until just tender, and carefully drained. The Danes serve asparagus in a folded napkin to keep it hot and to absorb any surplus moisture in the stalks. Hot asparagus is served with creamed butter, hollandaise, or cream sauce. Cold asparagus is served with a seasoned mayonnaise,* with horse-radish sauce with fresh cream,* or with vinaigrette.

Chicory with Prawns · *Endivie med Rejer*

18 small heads chicory
Boiling salted water
½ lb. cooked, shelled, and deveined prawns
3 oz. butter
1 oz. flour
16 fl. oz. single cream
Paprika

Cook the chicory in 1 inch of boiling salted water about 15 minutes, or until tender. Drain thoroughly and place in buttered shallow baking-dish. Place prawns on top of chicory. Melt butter and stir in flour. Cook over medium heat until blended, stirring constantly. Stir in the cream and cook, stirring constantly, until sauce is thickened and smooth. Pour sauce over chicory-prawn mixture and sprinkle with paprika. Place under grill until top is golden brown and bubbly.

Chicory with Ham · *Endivie med Skinke*

Proceed as above but substitute 2 to 3 cups diced ham for prawns.

Red Cabbage · *Rødkaal*

This is the most popular winter vegetable dish, and always served with roast goose at Christmas.

1 medium-sized red cabbage (about 3 lb.)
1½ oz. butter
1 tablespoon sugar or more, according to taste
2 fl. oz. vinegar
2 fl. oz. water
Salt
Pepper
2 medium-sized tart apples, peeled, cored, and chopped (optional)
5 oz. red currant jelly

Remove tough outer leaves from cabbage. Discard. Shred cabbage fine. In heavy pan, melt butter. Stir in sugar but do not brown. Add cabbage. Cook about 5 minutes, stirring constantly. Do not scorch. Add vinegar, water, salt and pepper to taste. Simmer, covered, over low heat for 2 to 3 hours, or until cabbage is very tender. Stir occasionally. If necessary, add a little more hot water, a tablespoon at a time, to prevent scorching. When cabbage is almost tender, add apples and red currant jelly. Taste cabbage. It should be sweet-sour; adjust taste with more sugar and vinegar, if necessary. Simmer, covered, for 30 minutes longer. Stir occasionally. Serve with roast meats, goose, or duck.

NOTE: *Red cabbage tastes better if made the day before using. Reheat slowly, stirring frequently.*

Sugar-browned Carrots · *Brunede Gulerødder*

4 to 6 medium carrots
1 oz. butter
1½ oz. sugar
½ teaspoon salt

Scrape carrots and cut into thin 3- to 4-inch strips. Cook in boiling salted water to cover until just tender. Drain thoroughly. Melt butter in frying-pan. When hot, stir in sugar. Cook, stirring constantly, until sugar is browned. Add boiled carrots and cook until golden on all sides, shaking frying-pan frequently. Do not scorch. Sprinkle with salt. Serve with meats or poultry, and accompany with a creamed vegetable, such as kale or spinach.

Cauliflower in Cheese Sauce

Blomkaal med Ostesauce

1 large cauliflower
4 eggs, separated
1 teaspoon sugar
Salt
Pepper
3 oz. grated cheese
12 fl. oz. medium white sauce

Trim cauliflower and break into flowerets. Cook in boiling salted water until barely tender. Butter a deep baking-dish. Beat egg yolks, sugar, salt and pepper to taste, and grated cheese into white sauce. Beat egg whites until stiff and fold into sauce. Place alternate layers of caulifowerets and sauce in baking-dish. Bake in 350° F., gas mark 4, oven about 20 minutes or until sauce is firm. Serve with creamed butter.

Hot Cauliflower with Prawns

Blomkaal med Rejer

A good main dish for lunch or supper.

2 oz. butter
4 tablespoons flour
8 fl. oz. milk
8 fl. oz. single or double cream
1 teaspoon salt
¼ teaspoon white pepper
4 fl. oz. double cream, whipped
1 large cauliflower
2 cups chopped cooked, shelled prawns
12 whole prawns

Melt butter and stir in flour. Gradually add milk and cream, stirring constantly. Cook over low heat, stirring all the time, until sauce is thick and smooth. Stir in salt and pepper, and fold in whipped cream. While making sauce, cook trimmed cauliflower whole in boiling salted water. Drain; place on hot plate and keep hot. Add prawns to sauce and heat thoroughly. Pour sauce over cauliflower and decorate with whole prawns.

Creamed Kale · *Grønlangkaal*

The Danes like kale and, cooked properly in the Danish manner, it is a far better vegetable than many people think.

2 lb. kale
1 teaspoon salt
Water
2 oz. butter
1 oz. flour
8 fl. oz. milk
8 fl. oz. single or double cream
½ teaspoon salt
½ teaspoon pepper

Remove tough stalks from kale. Wash and cut kale into bite-size pieces. Sprinkle with salt. Place in saucepan with enough water to cover. Bring to the boil and cook, covered, about 20 to 30 minutes, or until kale is tender. Drain and chop kale. Melt butter. Stir in flour. Gradually stir in milk and cream. Cook over low heat, stirring constantly, until smooth and thick. Add salt, pepper, and kale. Heat through thoroughly and serve with small sugar-browned potatoes* or sugar-browned carrots.*

Leeks · *Slikporrer*

Leeks are a popular Danish vegetable. Since they vary greatly in size, judge the quantity you need and cook the leeks as in the recipe below. Make sure that the leeks are approximately of the same size, so that they will all cook through in the same amount of time.

24 medium-sized leeks
2 teaspoons salt
Boiling water
4 oz. butter

Allow 4 leeks for each serving. Cut off the green tops and the roots. Rinse carefully several times in cold water to remove all sand. Tie leeks in bundles of 4. Place in a pan, sprinkle with salt, and add boiling water to cover. Simmer 10 to 15 minutes, or until leeks are tender. Drain thoroughly. Place on a hot platter and remove strings. Cream and whip the butter until white and soft. Top leeks with butter.

Mrs Jensen's Creamed Mushrooms

Svampe i Flødestuvning

1½ oz. butter
1 lb. mushrooms, sliced
8 fl. oz. double cream, hot
Salt
Paprika
2 dessertspoons sherry or madeira

Heat butter in heavy frying-pan. Add mushrooms and cook, uncovered, over medium heat for about 5 minutes. Shake pan frequently to avoid scratching. Remove from heat and stir in hot cream, salt and paprika to taste, and sherry or madeira. Serve immediately as a garnish, or on toast, or with omelets or scrambled eggs, or in hot patty shells.

Mushroom Soufflé · *Svampegratin*

½ lb. mushrooms, sliced
2 oz. butter
1 teaspoon grated onion
¾ oz. flour
8 fl. oz. single cream
4 eggs, separated
½ teaspoon salt
¼ teaspoon pepper

Sauté mushrooms in ½ oz. hot butter until barely cooked. Do not cover pan. Shake frequently to prevent scorching. Stir in grated onion. Remove from heat and reserve. Melt 1½ oz. butter and stir in flour. Gradually add cream, stirring constantly. Cook until thick and smooth, stirring all the time. Remove from heat and beat in egg yolks, one at a time, blending thoroughly. Season with salt and pepper. Add mushrooms and mix well. Beat egg whites until stiff but not dry. Egg whites should stand in stiff peaks. Do not overbeat. Fold egg whites gently into mushroom mixture. Pour into a greased or ungreased baking-dish. Bake in 375° F., gas mark 5, oven 30 to 40 minutes. Serve with hot hollandaise sauce. Makes 3 servings.

NOTE: *Though the ingredients in this recipe may be doubled, it is preferable to make two smaller soufflés rather than one large one. Adjust baking time for a larger soufflé – the mixture should barely test clean if a soft soufflé is wanted. For a more solid soufflé, bake a few minutes longer.*

Browned Onions · *Brunede Løg*

24 small white onions (the smaller the better)
4 oz. butter
1 teaspoon salt
2 oz. brown sugar

Cook onions in gently boiling water in their skins until tender. Drain, cool, and peel. (This avoids tears.) Melt butter in frying-pan. Stir in salt and brown sugar. Cook for 1 minute, stirring constantly. Add onions and cook over lowest possible heat until browned on all sides. Stir or shake frying-pan frequently to avoid sticking. Serve with meats and game.

Onions with Blue Cheese

18 small white onions
1 oz. butter
½ oz. flour
8 fl. oz. milk
3 dessertspoons crumbled Danish Blue cheese or more, to taste
Dash of cayenne

Cook unpeeled onions in gently boiling water to cover until tender. Peel. (This way of cooking onions avoids tears.) Melt butter. Stir in flour. Gradually add milk. Cook over low heat, stirring constantly, until thick and smooth. Stir in cheese and cayenne. Add onions to sauce. Heat over medium heat for about 4 to 5 minutes, stirring frequently. Serve with roast meats.

Peas and Carrots · *Aerter og Gulerødder*

6 carrots
24 fl. oz. water
3 lb. peas, shelled, or 2 10-oz. packages frozen peas
1 teaspoon salt
1 oz. butter
2½ oz. flour
Vegetable stock
½ teaspoon sugar
½ teaspoon salt
2 dessertspoons chopped parsley

Scrape carrots and cube. Add water and bring to the boil. Simmer for 5 minutes. Add peas and 1 teaspoon salt. Simmer 5 to 10 minutes longer, or until vegetables are tender. Drain and reserve vegetable stock. Melt butter and stir in flour. Measure 12 fl. oz. vegetable stock and stir gradually into butter and flour mixture. Cook over low heat, stirring constantly, until thick and smooth. Stir in sugar and ½ teaspoon salt. Add the vegetables. Heat through thoroughly. Place in hot vegetable-dish and sprinkle with parsley.

Sugar-browned Potatoes · *Brunede Kartofler*

This is the way the Danes like potatoes when they don't serve them boiled.

12 small new potatoes
1 oz. butter
3 dessertspoons sugar
1 teaspoon salt

Cook potatoes in boiling salted water until tender. Drain and peel. Melt butter in frying-pan. When hot, stir in sugar. Cook, stirring constantly, until sugar is browned. Add boiled potatoes and cook until browned on all sides, shaking the frying-pan frequently. Do not scorch. Sprinkle with salt and serve with meats, fowl, ham, or as part of a vegetable platter.

Potato and Apple Purée · *Kartoffelmos med Aebler*

A very old country dish, good with pork.

4 oz. butter
2 cups hot mashed potatoes
2 cups thick unsweetened apple sauce made from tart apples
1 oz. sugar
½ teaspoon nutmeg
½ teaspoon salt

Beat butter into hot potatoes. Add all other ingredients and check for taste. Add more sugar and salt if needed. Cool. Place in buttered baking-dish and swirl the mixture into peaks with a spoon. Bake in 400° F., gas mark 6, oven for 30 minutes, or until top is lightly browned.

Beet Salad with Cooked Dressing · *Rødbedesalat*

½ oz. butter
¼ oz. flour
8 fl. oz. bouillon
4 fl. oz. mild vinegar
½ teaspoon salt
¼ teaspoon pepper
½ teaspoon prepared mustard
1 teaspoon sugar
4 large beets, cooked
1 celeriac, cooked
Parsley sprigs

Melt butter and stir in flour. Gradually stir in bouillon. Cook over low heat, stirring constantly, until thickened and smooth. Stir in vinegar, salt, pepper, mustard, and sugar. Cool. Peel and dice beets and celeriac. Combine dressing and vegetables and mix thoroughly. Chill before serving. Garnish with parsley.

Pickled Beets · *Syltede Rødbeder*

These are used constantly on the cold table and as a relish for meats.

4 fl. oz. cider or wine vinegar
4 fl. oz. water
2 oz. sugar
1 teaspoon salt
$\frac{1}{4}$ teaspoon pepper
About 2 cups cooked, peeled, and thinly sliced beets
1 dessertspoon caraway seeds (optional)

Combine vinegar, water, sugar, salt, and pepper and bring to the boil. Cool. Place beets in deep bowl and pour dressing over them. Sprinkle with caraway seeds. Let stand for at least 9 hours before using. Drain before serving.

Celeriac Salad · *Sellerisalat*

Celeriacs are dark knobs that must be peeled before using. They taste much like celery, though more so, and are a great Danish favourite. Celeriac can be bought at most good vegetable markets and they are not expensive. This is a very popular Danish salad, and a good one.

3 medium-sized celeriacs
Water
Juice of $\frac{1}{2}$ lemon or vinegar
4 fl. oz. double cream, whipped
4 fl. oz. mayonnaise
1 teaspoon prepared mustard

Peel celeriac so that only white part shows. Cut into slivers about $\frac{1}{16}$ inch thick or as thin as you can make them. Do not use woody parts in the middle. Drop celeriac immediately into water combined with lemon juice or vinegar to prevent discolouring. Combine whipped cream, mayonnaise, and prepared mustard. Drain celeriac and fold into dressing. Chill for 2 hours or longer. Serve on a bed of lettuce.

Pickled Cucumbers · *Agurkesalat*

The universal Danish salad.

2 to 3 cucumbers
1 dessertspoon salt
6 fl. oz. cider or wine vinegar
1 dessertspoon sugar or more, according to taste
$\frac{1}{4}$ teaspoon white pepper
1 dessertspoon chopped parsley or dill

Scrub cucumbers free of waxy coating. Dry. Score with the prongs of a fork. Slice as thinly as possible, preferably with a vegetable slicer. The slices should be transparent. Place in deep bowl and sprinkle with salt. Cover with a plate and weigh down with something heavy. Let stand at room temperature 1 to 2 hours. Drain thoroughly and squeeze out remaining juice. Combine vinegar, sugar, and pepper. Pour over cucumbers. Taste for seasonings. Chill cucumbers thoroughly. At serving time, drain and sprinkle with parsley or dill.

Margrethe Schanne's Salad

1 cup unpeeled, cored, diced apples
4 large heads of chicory, sliced
⅓ cup blanched almonds, chopped
¼ cup soaked currants
½ cup mayonnaise
2 fl. oz. double cream, whipped
1 teaspoon sugar
White pepper

Combine apples, chicory, almonds, and currants. Mix together mayonnaise, whipped cream, and sugar. Combine fruit mixture and dressing. Season with white pepper to taste. Chill before serving. Serve with cold ham or other cold meats.

Variation: If this salad is to be served with cold roast beef, add a little horse-radish to taste.

Dannevang Salad

Dressing

5 fl. oz. olive oil
2½ fl. oz. tarragon vinegar
1 teaspoon salt
½ teaspoon pepper
1 teaspoon dry mustard

Salad

1¼ cups cubed Samsø or other Danish cheese
1¼ cups diced cooked chicken and ham, mixed
2 cups shredded lettuce
6 large ripe tomatoes

Combine all dressing ingredients and blend well. Toss cheese with chicken, ham, and lettuce, and toss salad with dressing. Chill. Cut tomatoes into halves. Scoop out the centre of each half. Fill tomatoes with chilled salad.

Gypsy Cheese Salad

Dressing

1 cup mayonnaise
½ teaspoon salt
¼ teaspoon pepper
¼ teaspoon paprika
1 teaspoon or more fresh or prepared horse-radish

Salad

1 cup cooked chilled green peas
2 cups diced boiled potatoes
1 cup Danish ham or salami, cut into julienne strips
1 cup cubed Samsø cheese
1 cup thinly sliced cucumbers
6 anchovy fillets
3 hard-boiled eggs, sliced

Combine all dressing ingredients and blend thoroughly. Combine all salad ingredients except anchovy fillets and hard-boiled egg slices. Toss salad with dressing. Spoon into salad bowl and chill. Garnish with anchovy fillets and egg slices.

Sauces

Sauces

Sauces (*saucer*), especially French ones, play an important role in Danish cooking, because practically every dish is served with a suitable sauce. Since all good standard English and French cookbooks feature recipes for such sauces as béarnaise, bordelaise, chasseur, hollandaise, mayonnaise, mousseline, remoulade, Robert, Valois, velouté, verte and au vin blanc, I have omitted them from this chapter.

The sauces that follow have a very Danish character, either in their composition (sauces made with whipped cream), their ingredients (horse-radish, mustard) or in their adaptation (Cumberland, soubise). Simple melted butter is often served along with a real sauce, especially in the case of fish.

Creamed Butter · *Rørt Smør*

This sauce is used on fish and vegetables. It can be varied in many ways, such as by adding a little curry powder, onion, garlic, mustard, horse-radish, parsley, or red wine.

Cream 6 oz. butter in a warm bowl until it is white and as thick as mayonnaise. Add a few drops of warm water to speed the creaming. If the sauce is to be used for fish, add lemon juice to taste and a little pepper.

Fish Sauces · *Fiskesaucer*

Cream sauce or béchamel, with a number of variations, is one of the most popular fish sauces in Denmark.

Cream Sauce

1 oz. butter
½ oz. flour
8 fl. oz. milk or fish stock, or a combination of both
Salt
Pepper
2 fl. oz. double cream or ½ oz. butter

Melt butter and stir in flour. Gradually add milk or fish stock, stirring constantly, and cook until sauce is thickened and smooth. Cook over lowest possible heat at least 5 minutes, stirring frequently, or cook in top of double boiler over simmering water 10 minutes. Season with salt and pepper to taste. Stir in cream or butter.

Curry Sauce (*Karrysauce*). Add 1 or more teaspoons curry powder to milk or fish stock.

Tomato Sauce (*Tomatsauce*). Add 2 to 3 teaspoons tomato sauce to cream sauce *before* adding the cream or butter.

Parsley Sauce (*Persillesauce*). Add $\frac{1}{4}$ cup minced parsley to cream sauce.

Prawn Sauce (*Rejesauce*). Add 1 cup chopped, cooked, shelled, and deveined prawns to cream sauce, and 2 tablespoons chopped dill.

Egg Sauce (*Aeggesauce*). Beat together 2 eggs and 2 fl. oz. vinegar. Add to cream sauce. Omit cream and use butter in finishing cream sauce. Add 2 dessertspoons chopped parsley or dill, and capers to taste, if desired.

Mornay Sauce (*Mornaysauce*). Add 1 beaten egg yolk and 1 oz. grated Swiss or Parmesan cheese to cream sauce.

Anchovy Sauce (*Ansjossauce*). Add 3 fillets of anchovies, minced, or 1 teaspoon or more anchovy paste to cream sauce.

Mustard Sauce (*Sennepssauce*). Add 2 or more teaspoons prepared mustard to cream sauce.

Horse-radish Sauce (*Peberrodsauce*). Add 1 teaspoon or more grated fresh horse-radish and $\frac{1}{4}$ teaspoon ground coriander (optional) to cream sauce.

Brown Sauce · *Brun Grundsauce*

This is the classic 'Espagnole' sauce, a cornerstone of fine cooking and the basis of many other sauces. The sauce *must* be cooked extremely slowly, and it should be stirred, never beaten.

4 oz. beef dripping
1 carrot, diced
1 onion, chopped
1 celery heart, chopped
1 crushed bay leaf
¼ cup chopped parsley
½ teaspoon dry thyme or 2 sprigs fresh thyme
1 dessertspoon chopped bacon
2 oz. flour
10 black peppercorns
2 cups drained peeled tomatoes
½ cup chopped parsley
3¼ pints strong clear beef bouillon

Melt beef dripping in heavy saucepan. Add carrot, onion, celery, bay leaf, ¼ cup chopped parsley, thyme, and bacon. Cook over high heat, stirring constantly, until mixture begins to brown. Sprinkle with flour. Cook, stirring constantly, until flour is well browned. Add all other ingredients. Simmer over lowest possible heat for about 3 hours, or until liquid is reduced to half. Skim as needed. Stir occasionally. Strain sauce and cool, stirring occasionally. Use as it is, correcting seasonings, or use as basis for other sauces. Makes about 2½ pints.

Brown Sauce with Fruit · *Brun Sauce med Frugt*

With Oranges (*med appelsin*). Add the peeled and membrane-free sections of 2 or 3 oranges to 12 to 16 fl. oz. brown sauce.* Heat through before serving. Serve with roast meat or chicken. Makes about 1 pint.

With Grapes (*med druer*). Add 1 cup peeled and seeded green grapes to 12 to 16 fl. oz. brown sauce.* Heat through before serving. Serve with game birds and venison. Makes about 1 pint.

Madeira Sauce · *Madeirasauce*

12 fl. oz. brown sauce*
4 fl. oz. madeira or dry sherry
1½ oz. unsalted butter, in small pieces
2 dessertspoons madeira or dry sherry

Heat sauce and cook until reduced by one third. Stir in 4 fl. oz. madeira or sherry and heat through. Add butter piece by piece, stirring until each addition has melted. Do not allow to boil after butter has been added, or the flavour of the sauce will be spoiled. Stir in 2 dessertspoons madeira before serving. Use with all meats, fowl, and game. Makes about 12 fl. oz.

NOTE: *The sauce may be made in the pan in which meat has been roasted, to utilize the pan juices.*

Danish Soubise Sauce

This sauce is infinitely superior to all other soubise sauces, thanks to the cognac and the port. I am indebted for it to Mrs Gertie Wandell, Member of Parliament and fomenter of many good causes.

3 large onions, sliced as thinly as possible
2 oz. butter
2 fl. oz. cognac
1 dessertspoon flour
½ teaspoon salt
¼ teaspoon white pepper
6 fl. oz. chicken broth
3 dessertspoons good port
2–3 fl. oz. double cream

In heavy saucepan, cook onions in 1 oz. butter for 15 minutes. Cook over lowest possible heat, stirring occasionally. Do not let onions colour. Add cognac and sprinkle with flour, salt, and pepper and cook 3 minutes longer, stirring constantly. Add chicken broth and simmer, covered, over lowest possible heat 1¼ hours. Keep mixture as white as possible. Rub through fine sieve or purée in blender. Place in top of double boiler and stir in port and cream. Add 1 oz. butter and stir until melted. Serve with poached chicken breasts, poached fish or sea-food, or roast duck and other game birds.

Mayonnaise with Horse-radish

Mayonnaise med Peberrod

6 fl. oz. mayonnaise
2 to 4 teaspoons fresh grated or bottled horse-radish
3 dessertspoons double cream

Combine all ingredients and blend thoroughly. Serve with fish or on smørrebrød.

Cumberland Sauce 1

¼ cup red currant jelly or more
1 dessertspoon tart vinegar
2 fl. oz. port
2–3 fl. oz. dry red wine
Juice of ½ orange
1 teaspoon grated onion
2 teaspoons grated orange rind
1 teaspoon English mustard
Salt
Pepper
⅛ teaspoon ground ginger

Melt red currant jelly and cool. Blend in all other ingredients. Serve cold or heat again to serve hot.

Cumberland Sauce 2

8 fl. oz. brown sauce*
¼ cup red currant jelly*
2 fl. oz. dry red wine
3 dessertspoons dry sherry

Combine all ingredients and heat through. Serve with ham.

Horse-radish Sauce with Fresh Cream

Peberrodsauce med Fløde

For fish, lobster, shrimp, chicken, aspics, and mixed vegetable salads.

2 fl. oz. wine vinegar
8 fl. oz. double cream, whipped
3 dessertspoons grated fresh horse-radish
Salt
Pepper
1 dessertspoon chopped parsley, chives, or dill (optional)

Stir vinegar into whipped cream. When mixture has reached the consistency of mayonnaise, add horse-radish and salt and pepper to taste. Sprinkle with chopped parsley, chives, or dill.

Variation 1: For a blander sauce, favoured by many Danes, omit vinegar.

Variation 2: If bottled horse-radish is used, omit vinegar and use 3 parts whipped cream to 1 part bottled horse-radish. Season with salt and pepper to taste.

Sour Cream Sauce · *Sur Flødesauce*

A sauce for fish and sea-food.

1 raw egg yolk
1 hard-boiled egg, chopped
¾ teaspoon sugar
½ teaspoon salt
¼ teaspoon white pepper
½ teaspoon mild prepared mustard
2 teaspoons lemon juice
8 fl. oz. sour cream

Combine all ingredients and blend thoroughly. Check seasonings and chill before serving.

Mustard Sauce with Whipped Cream

Sennepssauce med Fløde

For fish and sea-food.

1 hard-boiled egg yolk
1 raw egg yolk
2 teaspoons Dijon or other prepared mustard
2 dessertspoons wine vinegar
Salt
Pepper
8 fl. oz. double cream, whipped

Combine all ingredients (with salt and pepper to taste) except whipped cream, and blend thoroughly. Fold into whipped cream. Serve immediately.

Remoulade Sauce for Fried Fish

8 fl. oz. mayonnaise
¼ cup finely chopped sour pickles
1 dessertspoon finely chopped drained capers
1½ teaspoons parsley
1½ teaspoons dried tarragon
1½ teaspoons dried chervil

Combine all ingredients and blend thoroughly. Though it is not necessary, the flavour of the tarragon and chervil is improved by soaking the herbs for 5 minutes in 1 dessertspoon of water each. Squeeze dry before using. Makes about 8 fl. oz. sauce.

Sharp Sauce · *Skarp Sauce*

For *gravlaks* and boiled or fried fish.

9 dessertspoons olive oil
3 dessertspoons wine vinegar
2 to 3 dessertspoons sharp prepared mustard
¾ teaspoon salt
¼ teaspoon freshly ground pepper
1½ oz. sugar
⅛ teaspoon cardamom

Combine ingredients and blend thoroughly. Chill sauce for several hours. At serving time, beat smooth with fork or wire whisk – do not use rotary beater. Makes about 8 fl. oz.

Meat Aspic · *Gelé*

For fish, shrimps, lobster, tongue, and any meats.

24 fl. oz. clear chicken bouillon
5 fl. oz. tomato juice
4 dessertspoons unflavoured gelatin
Salt
Pepper
2 egg shells, crushed
2 egg whites, lightly beaten
2 dessertspoons cognac or madeira

Combine all ingredients except cognac and heat slowly, stirring constantly until mixture comes to the boil. Strain through a sieve lined with a triple layer of muslin or a kitchen cloth that has been wrung out in cold water. Stir in cognac. Chill before using. Makes about 1½ pints.

Desserts

Desserts

Every Dane seems to be born with a sweet tooth, and it is heart-warming to see a modern Viking put away his third helping of a delicious whipped cream confection, either as a dessert after a meal, or at an afternoon coffee party, or during the evening.

There is a considerable difference between everyday family desserts and party desserts. The first are on the simple side, consisting of seasonal fruits stewed and thickened with a little cornflour, or enriched with a little meringue. Dessert can also be pancakes or French toast. Party desserts, on the other hand, are gorgeous creams, layer cakes filled with custards, jams, macaroons, and whipped cream, topped with meringues or other utterly rich, utterly devastating, and utterly irresistible creations. And of course there are the Danish pastries and all the other pastries that fall between a dessert and a cake.

It must be stressed that all Danish desserts, including the simplest ones, are beautiful to look at, like all Danish food. It is with a sigh of regret that one demolishes these sweet works of art – but one invariably does.

Moulded Cream Ring with Fruit

Fløderand med Henkogte Frugter

Very easy and very handsome.

3 eggs, separated
4 oz. sugar
1 teaspoon vanilla
2 dessertspoons unflavoured gelatin
2 fl. oz. milk
16 fl. oz. double cream, whipped
Stewed fruit or frozen fruit, thawed

Beat egg yolks with sugar and vanilla until thick and lemon-coloured. Dissolve gelatin in milk over hot water. Stir into egg mixture. Fold in whipped cream. Whip egg whites until they stand in peaks and fold into mixture. Rinse 2 or 3 pint ring mould with cold water. Sprinkle inside with sugar. Spoon in cream. Chill until set. Unmould and fill ring with any stewed fruit or thawed frozen friut.

Red Fruit Pudding · *Rødgrød*

Perhaps the most popular of all Danish puddings and most refreshing. It can be made with one kind of berries only, but it is better to mix them. This pudding should not be as stiff as a gelatin pudding.

¾ lb. red currants or red and black currants mixed
¾ lb. raspberries
12 fl. oz. water or 6 fl. oz. water and 6 fl. oz. dry white wine, mixed
1 cup sugar
¼ teaspoon salt
⅓ cup cornflour
8 fl. oz. water
⅓ cup blanched almonds, slivered
Cream

Trim and gently wash fruit. Drain; place in deep frying-pan with the 12 fl. oz. water or water and wine mixed. Simmer, covered, 10 minutes. Strain through a fine sieve. Measure juice and, if necessary, add water to make 20 fl. oz. liquid. Add sugar and salt. Bring to boiling point, stirring constantly. Mix cornflour with 4 fl. oz. water to a smooth paste. Stir into fruit juice. Bring to the boil and cook 3 minutes, stirring constantly. Remove from heat. Pour into glass serving-dish and chill. Decorate with slivered almonds. Serve with cream.

NOTE: *To serve in the Danish manner, rinse cereal bowls with cold water and sprinkle with sugar. Pour individual helpings of* rødgrød. *Sprinkle with sugar to prevent skin from forming and decorate with almond slivers.*

Red Fruit Pudding made with Frozen Berries

Rødgrød

Very worth making when fresh berries are not available.

2 10-oz. packages frozen raspberries, thawed
2 10-oz. packages frozen strawberries, thawed
⅓ cup cornflour
4 fl. oz. water
1 dessertspoon lemon juice
Sugar
⅓ cup blanched almonds, slivered
Cream

Combine berries in saucepan. Bring to the boil, stirring occasionally. Strain through fine sieve or purée in blender. Mix cornflour with 4 fl. oz. water to a smooth paste. Bring fruit back to boiling point. Stir cornflour into fruit. Bring to the boil and cook 3 minutes, stirring constantly. Remove from heat and blend in lemon juice. Pour into glass serving dish and sprinkle top with a little sugar. Chill. Decorate with slivered almonds before serving. Serve with cream.

Rhubarb Pudding · *Rabarbergrød*

The pudding that greets the spring.

2 lb. rhubarb, trimmed and cut in ½-in. pieces
1 lb. 6 oz. sugar
Water
3 dessertspoons cornflour
2 fl. oz. water
1 teaspoon vanilla
Cream

Sprinkle rhubarb with sugar. Add water to cover. Bring to the boil. Cover and simmer until rhubarb is soft. Mix cornflour with water to a smooth paste. Stir into rhubarb. Cook, stirring constantly, until thick and clear. Stir in vanilla. Pour into glass serving-dish and sprinkle pudding with sugar. Chill and serve with double cream.

Lemon Delight · '*Kan ikke lade vaere*'

A refreshing dessert, good for a heavy meal.

5 eggs, separated
4 oz. sugar
2 dessertspoons unflavoured gelatin
2 fl. oz. cold water
Juice and grated rind of 2 lemons

Beat egg yolks with sugar until very thick and lemon-coloured. Soften gelatin in cold water for 5 minutes. Heat over hot water, stirring until gelatin is dissolved. Add gelatin to lemon juice and lemon rind. Stir lemon mixture gradually into egg mixture. Blend thoroughly. Beat egg whites until they stand in peaks. Fold egg whites into lemon mixture. Pour into a rinsed bowl or serving dish. Chill until set. Serve covered with whipped cream or with a fruit sauce.

NOTE: *This dessert improves upon standing for 1 day in the refrigerator, or in a cold larder.*

Rum Pudding · *Rom-fromage*

6 egg yolks
7–8 oz. sugar
2 dessertspoons unflavoured gelatin
5 fl. oz. cold water
½ cup blanched almonds, slivered
2–3 fl. oz. rum
16 fl. oz. double cream, whipped

Beat egg yolks until light. Beat in sugar, 2 dessertspoons at a time, beating well after each addition. Soften gelatin in cold water and dissolve over hot water. Pour gelatin into egg mixture, stirring constantly. Stir in almond slivers and rum. Chill until mixture begins to thicken. Fold in whipped cream. Pour into rinsed mould and chill until set. Unmould and serve with raspberry sauce* or any other fruit sauce.

Mrs Johannes Laursen's Orange Soufflé

Appelsin Fromage

Excellent.

3 eggs, separated
4 oz. sugar
2 dessertspoons grated orange rind
6 fl. oz. strained fresh orange juice
1 dessertspoon unflavoured gelatin
2 fl. oz. water
16 fl. oz. double cream, whipped

Beat egg yolks until light. Beat in sugar, a dessertspoon at a time, beating well after each addition. Stir in grated orange rind and orange juice. Soften gelatin in cold water and dissolve over hot water. Add to egg mixture, blending thoroughly. Chill until mixture begins to thicken. Fold in double cream and stiffly beaten egg whites. Spoon into glass serving-dish and chill until set. Decorate top with drained tinned mandarin orange slices and more whipped cream, if desired.

Mrs Johannes Laursen's Caramel Pudding

Kardmelrand

½ lb. sugar
4 fl. oz. hot water
6 eggs, separated
2 oz. sugar
⅘ pint double cream, heated
½ teaspoon vanilla
⅖ pint double cream, whipped
2 dessertspoons brandy

Melt sugar in heavy frying-pan. Stir until sugar is browned, but do not scorch. Pour two-thirds of the caramel into the bottom of a warmed 2½ pint ring mould. Add water to remaining syrup. Stir constantly over low heat until liquid and smooth. Beat egg yolks with sugar. Gradually beat in heated cream and vanilla. Stir mixture until cooled. Beat egg whites until they stand in stiff peaks and fold into egg mixture. Pour into mould. Place mould in a baking-pan with enough water to come up ⅓ the height of the mould, or about 1 inch. Bake in 350° F., gas mark 4, oven 45 minutes to 1 hour, or until set. Chill. Combine whipped cream and brandy. Unmould pudding and fold the cooled caramel sauce into the whipped cream. Serve on pudding or separately.

Princess Pudding · *Prinsessesbudding*

4 oz. butter
4 oz. sifted plain flour
12 fl. oz. single cream or milk, heated
1 teaspoon vanilla
6 eggs, separated
5 dessertspoons sugar
1 teaspoon ground cardamom
Dry breadcrumbs

Melt butter and stir in flour. Cook, stirring constantly, about 3 minutes. Gradually add hot single cream or milk, beating with electric beater. When mixture is well blended and smooth, remove from heat and stir in vanilla and egg yolks, one at a time. Beat at least 5 minutes with an electric beater or 10 minutes by hand after the last yolk has been added. (The Danish recipe specifies 20 minutes.) Beat in sugar and cardamom. Beat egg whites until they stand in stiff peaks and fold into mixture. Sprinkle a well-buttered 3-pint mould with dry breadcrumbs. Spoon in batter. Cover with lid or make a lid with aluminium foil and tie it with string. Place mould in large saucepan with simmering water ⅔ up the sides of the mould. Simmer for about 1½ hours, replenishing water as needed. Do not use boiling water, but barely simmering water only, or pudding will have holes. Unmould carefully and serve with a red fruit sauce or a cherry compote.

Veiled Country Lass · *Bondepige med Slør*

Very good, but the dish must be made with pumpernickel or very dark rye bread.

4 cups finely grated, very dry pumpernickel or rye breadcrumbs
1½ oz. butter, in pieces
1 oz. sugar
2 cups thick apple sauce
12 fl. oz. double cream, whipped
2 dessertspoons raspberry jam or currant jelly

Combine breadcrumbs, butter, and sugar in heavy frying-pan. Sauté over medium heat, stirring constantly, until the breadcrumbs are very crisp. Cool mixture. Place alternate layers of breadcrumbs and apple sauce in serving-dish, ending with breadcrumbs. Cover top with whipped cream. Decorate with raspberry jam or currant jelly. Chill before serving.

Variation 1: Substitute for one layer of apple sauce a layer of raspberry jam or currant jelly.

Variation 2: Add 1 to 2 dessertspoons grated chocolate to toasted breadcrumbs. Use semi-sweet or sweet baking chocolate.

Henry Birkshoj's Apple Meringue

Three generations of Birkshoj men work at the Tuborg Breweries. Henry has been there for over fifty years, combining an interest in beer with one in good food.

4 egg whites
½ teaspoon cream of tartar
1⅔ cups sifted icing sugar
⅔ cup blanched almonds, finely ground
½ teaspoon almond extract
4 cups thick, well-flavoured apple sauce or apple compote, made from tart apples
Whipped cream

Beat egg whites until foamy. Beat in cream of tartar. Beat in icing sugar, 1 or 2 dessertspoons at a time. Fold in almonds and almond extract. Place apple sauce in buttered 3-pint dish. Top with meringue. Bake in 275° F., gas mark 1, oven about 30 to 45 minutes, or until barely golden in colour. Serve warm or cold, with whipped cream.

NOTE: *The success of this dessert depends on the apple sauce. If it is insipid or too sweet, the dessert will suffer.*

Rødvig Kro Apple Tart

Aebletaerte med Crème Fraîche

Tart

4 oz. butter
4 oz. sugar
2 egg yolks
½ teaspoon almond extract
1¼ cups sifted plain flour

Filling

12 fl. oz. single cream
2-inch piece vanilla pod
4 oz. sugar
1 oz. flour
4 egg yolks, well beaten
4 fl. oz. double cream, whipped
3 large well-flavoured apples, on the tart side
Salted water
6 oz. sugar or more, depending on tartness of apples
12 fl. oz. double cream, whipped

To make *tart*, cream butter with sugar until fluffy. Beat in egg yolks, one at a time, beating well after each addition. Stir in almond extract. Beat in flour. Pat dough into bottom and sides of 9- or 10-inch round spring-form pan or deep pie-pan. Use preferably a pan with a detachable bottom since the tart cannot be unmoulded. Bake in 350° F., gas mark 4, oven about 30 minutes. Cool.

To make *filling*, scald single cream with vanilla bean. In top of double boiler, beat together sugar, flour, and egg yolks until smooth. Place over (not into) simmering water. Remove vanilla bean from scalded cream and add cream gradually to egg mixture, stirring constantly. Cook, stirring constantly, until mixture just reaches boiling point. Remove from heat and cool, stirring frequently. Fold whipped cream into cold custard.

Spoon cold custard into cooled tart. Peel and core apples, and cut into thin slices. Drop slices into salted water to prevent discoloration. Drain and dry apple slices and pile on custard in the shape of a dome. Preheat oven to 450° F., gas mark 8. Sprinkle sugar over apples. Place in oven just long enough to melt sugar. Pipe whipped cream over apples in decorative designs. Makes about 8 to 10 servings.

Apple Cake · *Aeblekage*

Not a cake in our sense of the word, but the most popular of all Danish desserts. There are any number of variations, and the crumbs may be either breadcrumbs, or made from zwieback, cake, cookies, macaroons, or a combination of any two. Personally, I prefer fine dry breadcrumbs.

4 oz. butter
1 tablespoon sugar
2½ cups crumbs
4 cups thick, well-flavoured apple sauce, made with tart apples
8 fl. oz. double cream, whipped and sweetened to taste

Heat butter and stir in sugar. Brown crumbs in mixture until crisp. Place alternate layers of crumbs and apple sauce in serving-dish, beginning and ending with a layer of crumbs. Chill. Before serving, decorate with swirls of whipped cream. Or place layers in well-buttered 2½ pint baking-dish or spring-form pan. Bake in 350° F., gas mark 4, oven about 45 minutes to 1 hour. Cool, unmould, and decorate with whipped cream.

NOTE: *For a richer cake, place macaroons between layers of crumbs and apple sauce. The macaroons may be soaked in sherry or madeira.*

Jørgen Ranten's Variation: Proceed as above, but use fresh strawberries, blackberries, or raspberries, sweetened to taste, instead of the apple sauce.

Fancy Danish Apple Cake · *Fin Aeblekage*

3 medium-sized tart apples
2 fl. oz. Cherry Heering
3 oz. sugar
2 cups dry almond macaroon crumbs
½ teaspoon nutmeg
3 oz. butter
Custard sauce* or whipped cream

Pare, core, and dice apples. Combine apples, Cherry Heering and sugar in saucepan. Simmer, covered, over low heat, stirring occasionally, until apples are tender. Mix macaroon crumbs with nutmeg. Heat butter in frying-pan and brown macaroon crumbs in it over moderate heat. Stir layers of crumbs and apples in buttered baking-dish, or 7-inch buttered spring-form pan, beginning and ending with macaroon crumbs. Bake in 350° F., gas mark 4, oven about 30 minutes. Cool and unmould. Serve with custard sauce or whipped cream.

Mrs Arne Christiansen's Fruit Salad · *Frugt Salat*

2 cups mixed fresh fruit, such as apples, pears, grapes, bananas, oranges, apricots, peaches, and sweet stoned cherries
Lemon juice
2 eggs, beaten
1½ oz. sugar
1 teaspoon vanilla
Juice of 1 lemon
Juice of 1 orange
4 fl. oz. double cream, whipped
Walnut halves
Maraschino cherries

Wash, dry, and prepare fruit, slicing thinly or dicing when necessary. If the peel is thin and crisp, the fruit does not need to be peeled. Sprinkle fruit with a little lemon juice to prevent discolouring. Combine eggs, sugar, vanilla, lemon and orange juice. Blend thoroughly. Cook in top of double-boiler over simmering (not boiling) water until mixture is thickened and smooth. Do not let boil; stir constantly. Cool, stirring occasionally. When cold, fold in whipped cream and fruits. Chill. Decorate with walnut halves and Maraschino cherries.

Katherine Plum Cake · *Katherineblommekage*

A dessert.

1 lb. prunes
12 fl. oz. water
12 fl. oz. port
4 large eggs, separated
4 oz. sugar
16 fl. oz. double cream, heated
1 teaspoon vanilla
4 oz. butter, melted
Juice of 1 lemon
About ⅔ cup blanched almonds or more
4 fl. oz. double cream, whipped

Soak prunes in water and port about 30 minutes. Simmer until tender. Let cool in liquid. While prunes are cooking, beat egg yolks with sugar until thick and white. Stir in hot cream and vanilla. For a smoother cream, strain through a fine strainer. Beat in melted butter and lemon juice. Beat egg whites until stiff. Fold into egg mixture. Drain cooled prunes. With the point of a sharp knife, carefully remove stones. Replace stones with almonds. Place prunes at the bottom of a well-buttered baking-dish. Spoon custard over prunes. Place baking-dish in a pan with about 1½ inches of water. Bake in 325° F., gas mark 3, oven about 1 hour, or until set. Chill and garnish with whipped cream before serving.

Wine Jelly from Steensgaard · *Portgelé*

2 dessertspoons unflavoured gelatin
4 fl. oz. water
8 fl. oz. fresh orange juice
⅘ pint claret or port
1 dessertspoon lemon juice
Sugar to taste
Whipped cream

Soften gelatin in cold water and dissolve over hot water. Combine orange juice, wine, and lemon juice. Add sugar to taste; if the wine is sweet, no sugar is needed. Stir in dissolved gelatin. Pour into glass serving-dish and chill until set. Serve with whipped cream.

Banana Desserts · *Banan Desserter*

Using their imagination, the Danes often make charming and quick desserts from bananas. Here are some ideas:

Peel bananas and cut into slices lengthwise. Sprinkle with

lemon juice to avoid discolouring. Pipe with swirls or rosettes of whipped cream. Top either with Maraschino cherries, halved and grated walnuts, peeled and seeded grapes, or teaspoonfuls of jam.

Or cut peeled bananas into 2- to 3-inch pieces and sprinkle with lemon juice. Stand on a bed of whipped cream and top with half a canned apricot or peach.

Or peel yellow and white skins from oranges. Cut oranges into thick slices and remove centre membrane and seeds, leaving a round hole. Pipe whipped cream around hole. Stand 3-inch banana pieces in hole and top each piece with a swirl of whipped cream. Sliced pineapple may be used instead of oranges.

Frozen Cream · *Frossen Fløde*

16 fl. oz. double cream, whipped
½ teaspoon vanilla
1 dessertspoon sugar
Fresh fruit or tinned fruit

Combine whipped cream with vanilla and sugar. Blend thoroughly. Spoon into refrigerator freezing tray and freeze until firm. Arrange mounds of fresh or tinned fruits, peeled and sliced or diced (pineapple, peaches, raspberries, strawberries, apples, pears, etc.), on serving-platter. Dip a serving-spoon into hot water and spoon out frozen cream. Arrange frozen cream spoonfuls around fruit and serve immediately.

NOTE: Gyldendals Store Kogebook, *a majestic volume of 563 pages, and one of the best and most complete cookbooks any nation has produced, follows this recipe with the remark that this frozen cream can be blended with horse-radish and served with cold roast beef or cold tongue. I would suggest that in this case the vanilla be omitted.*

Raspberry Sauce · *Hindbaer-sauce*

The same sauce can also be made with strawberries.

2 cups raspberries
3 oz. sugar
1 dessertspoon cornflour
1 dessertspoon water
1 dessertspoon cognac or rum

Combine raspberries with sugar and bring to boiling point, stirring frequently. Strain through a sieve or purée in blender. Add more sugar if necessary. Mix cornflour and water to a smooth paste. Heat raspberry purée and stir in cornflour. Cook, stirring constantly, until thickened and clear. Cool and stir in cognac or rum.

Frozen Raspberry Sauce

Purée two packets frozen raspberries, thawed, in blender, or push through a fine sieve. Stir in cognac or rum to taste.

Danish Custard Sauce · *Likørsauce*

3 egg yolks
1 oz. sugar
4 fl. oz. Cherry Heering
4 fl. oz. double cream

In top of double-boiler, combine egg yolks and sugar. Beat until thick. Beat in Cherry Heering and cream. Place over simmering (not boiling) water and cook, stirring constantly, until sauce coats the spoon. Serve warm over Danish apple cake.* Makes about ½ pint sauce.

Glacé Red Currants · *Glacé Ribs*

Very decorative for any dessert, but they must be eaten the day they are made.

Wash red currant clusters but do not stem. Place on paper towels and blot dry. (If not thoroughly dried, the fruit will not take the glaze.) Whip whites of egg as stiffly as possible. Dip currant clusters into beaten egg white. Shake off surplus egg white carefully. Place on baking sheets lined with kitchen towels. Sprinkle with confectioners' sugar. Dry completely. Shake off surplus sugar before serving.

Christmas Rice Porridge · *Jule Risengrød*

This is part of the Danish Christmas dinner, and in less abundant times the canny Danish housewives served it before their roast duck, goose, or pork. A whole blanched almond is put into the dish, and the person who gets the almond gets a prize. On Christmas Eve a dish of *risengrød* is set out in the open for the hobgoblins, and invariably the morning finds the dish empty.

1 lb. long-grain rice
Boiling water
4 pints milk
½ teaspoon salt
1 whole blanched almond
3 oz. unsalted butter
1 teaspoon cinnamon
4 oz. sugar
Raspberry juice or syrup or sweet non-alcoholic beer

Scald rice with boiling water, drain, and repeat process. Heat milk, preferably in top of double-boiler. When hot, stir in rice gradually so that the milk doesn't stop simmering. Cover tightly and cook over barely boiling water or over lowest possible heat until rice is extremely tender. Stir occasionally, and watch for scorching. Stir in salt, and blanched almond. Serve in heated bowls. Place a dessertspoon of butter on top of each serving. Combine cinnamon and sugar over porridge. The raspberry juice or syrup (diluted with water to taste) or heated beer may be poured over the porridge or drunk separately.

Baking

Marzipan Squares
Almond Macaroons
Almond Paste Confections
  Marzipan Pigs or Mice
  Walnuts
  Raspberry Balls
  Rum Cherries
How to Dip Marzipan Confections in Chocolate
Kringle
Cones with Whipped Cream
  Mrs A. W. Nielsen's Kraemmerhuse Variation
Kringler
Vanilla Wreaths
Anna Thompsen's Vanilla Rings
Mrs A. W. Nielsen's Finnish Bread
Mrs A. W. Nielsen's Horns
Sand Tarts
Love Rings
Specier
Currant Cookies
Medals
Mrs Peter Heering's Klejner
Mrs Peter Heering's Brown Cakes
Mrs Rasmussen's Brown Cookies
Peppernuts
Butter Cream for Small Cakes
Thick Vanilla Custard or Filling
White Icing
Milk Glaze
Thin Water, Orange, Lemon, Brandy, or Rum Icing

Baking Tips

Danish cakes are rich and close-grained, and if iced at all, it is with a thin sugar icing. These cakes are eaten with coffee, but then all Danish tortes, layer cakes, and cookies are served with coffee.

Only Swedish women bake more than Danish women. Baked goodies are an integral part of Danish eating and entertaining. No self-respecting Danish woman would like to be caught without a variety of cookies and a cake or two to take care of unexpected visitors, not to mention the demands of her family.

Though home-baking can be extremely fancy, Danish women are not expected to produce all the glories of Danish baking at home. There is a whole category of cakes called 'pastry-shop cakes' (konditorkager), which includes puff-paste confections, big and small party cakes, and almond paste confections. All of them are devastatingly beautiful, and bought as a matter of course in the *konditorier*, or pastry shops. On Sundays especially, Danish husbands are seen hurrying home with little white boxes full of cake for the afternoon coffee. Many of these cakes require a skill beyond that of the home cook, and I have had to omit them from this book. Alas, I've had to leave out other splendid cakes and cookies, or this would have become a book on Danish baking.

I have also left out Danish bread recipes. Our flours are different from Danish flours, and thus produce a different bread. Also, the Danes eat rye and whole wheat grain breads far oftener than we do, and these kinds of breads are better bought than made at home.

Baking

The leitmotiv of Danish baking is almonds, ground or used in almond paste. Though almond paste can be bought in delicatessen stores, it is easily made at home. The almonds should be ground in a nut grinder or, better still because it involves no effort, in an electric blender.

When you grind almonds or nuts, grind only a small quantity at a time. This way, they will stay dry and not get oily. Oily ground-nuts are not suitable for baking. (For this reason nuts should not be ground in a meat mincer.) If you plan to do a lot of Danish baking, I strongly advocate grinding nuts in a blender. It saves hours of work.

Potato starch is often used in Danish baking to give the product a drier texture. Cornflour makes an acceptable substitute, and this is what I have used in the recipes in this book.

Ammonium carbonate, the substitute for the 'hartshorn salt' which is indigenous to all Scandinavian baking, gives cakes and cookies a wonderfully crisp and light texture. It can be bought at all chemists, and if it comes in chips it should be ground to a powder. This is done by placing it between two sheets of waxed paper and using a rolling pin. It can be substituted for baking powder measure for measure, but I think it is better used in cookies than in cakes, generally speaking. Do not be put off by the odour of ammonia. The baked foods will have no trace of it.

Finally, this is MOST IMPORTANT and cannot be repeated too often, THE SUCCESS OF ALL BAKING DEPENDS ON A PREHEATED OVEN. It takes from 10 to 20 minutes to heat an oven properly. Have your ovens tested at least once a year for accuracy, since all ovens tend to go off. And when in doubt use an oven thermometer.

Layer Cakes · *Lagkage*

Danish layer cakes consist of many thin, crisp layers sandwiched together with a great variety of fillings. The idea is to contrast the crispness of the pastry with the creaminess of the filling.

The three recipes that follow are representative of the many others that exist in Danish cooking. It takes a certain amount of practice to bake layers that are very thin and even, and I would recommend that a hostess practice them on her family before attempting them for a party. This is well worth while, because nothing looks and tastes as impressive as a tower of wafer-thin and crisp layers with their glorious fillings.

Layer Cake Pastry 1 · *Lagkagebunde 1*

This recipe makes 6 to 8 round 8-inch layers. The cake's texture is fine-grained, resembling somewhat the classic French *génoise*. The ammonium carbonate makes for greater crispness.

5 oz. butter
1 cup sugar
4 eggs
1 teaspoon vanilla or other flavouring (optional)
2½ cups sifted plain flour
1 teaspoon ammonium carbonate (hartshorn) or baking powder

Cream butter and sugar at least 10 minutes by hand, or at least 5 minutes with electric beater at medium speed. (This makes for a fine texture.) The mixture should be thick and white. Add eggs one at a time, beating well after each addition. Stir in vanilla or other flavouring. Sift together flour and ammonium carbonate (see page 165.) Beat flour into egg mixture and blend thoroughly. Dough will be soft. Chill for 30 minutes to 1 hour. Cut 6 to 8 8-inch rounds from heavy waxed paper. Spread the soft dough thinly and evenly on waxed paper rounds, leaving about ½ inch space around the edge to allow expansion during baking. Use a broad knife frequently dipped in water. Place two rounds on one baking-sheet or more if the sheet will hold them. Bake in preheated 425° F., gas mark 7, oven about 8 to 10 minutes, depending on thickness of layers, or until golden brown at the edges. Do not overbake. Remove at once from hot baking sheets. Cool but do not remove the waxed paper until putting together the final cake. Store in an airtight container.

Layer Cake Pastry 2 · *Lagkagebunde 2*

This recipe makes 6 round 9-inch layers. The texture is brittle, along the lines of a very crisp pastry dough.

2 cups sifted plain flour
8 oz. cold butter
Iced water
3 oz. sugar

Sift flour into mixing-bowl. With pastry cutter or two knives, cut in butter until pieces are the size of peas. While mixing with fork, add 4 dessertspoons iced water gradually. Toss until dough just holds together. With cold hands, and handling as little as possible, shape into a ball. Chill for 30 minutes to 1 hour. Divide chilled dough into 6 portions. Use one portion at a time; keep others in refrigerator until used. Roll each portion between two sheets of waxed paper to a

9-inch round. Use a 9-inch layer cake-pan to measure round, and trim off excess dough. Slide each layer on to a baking-sheet and carefully peel off the top sheet of waxed paper. Prick with fork all over, or layers will shrink during baking. Brush layers with iced water and sprinkle each with 1 dessertspoon sugar. Bake in 425° F., gas mark 7, oven about 6 to 8 minutes, or until golden brown. Cool on baking-sheets. Carefully peel off the bottom waxed paper sheet before using.

Layer Cake Pastry 3 · *Lagkagebunde 3*

This recipe makes 6 round 8-inch layers. The layers are very thin and very crisp.

8 oz. butter
7 oz. sugar
8 oz. flour

Cream butter and sugar 10 minutes by hand or 4 to 5 minutes with electric beater at medium speed. Beat in flour and work with hands until dough is a smooth ball. Divide into 6 portions. Roll out each portion between 2 sheets of waxed paper to make an 8-inch round. Remove top waxed paper sheet but leave on bottom one. Place rounds on baking-sheets. Prick the entire surface with fork. Bake in 425° F., gas mark 7, oven about 6 minutes, or until golden brown. Remove from baking-sheets but do not remove waxed paper until the cake is to be assembled.

Cinnamon Layer Cake · *Kanellagkage*

A popular layer cake, on the simple side.

1 recipe layer cake pastry 3*
2 teaspoons cinnamon
16 fl. oz. double cream, whipped and sweetened to taste
1½ oz. semi-sweet chocolate, melted
1 cup blanched toasted almonds, chopped fine

Make layer cake pastry as directed, but add the 2 teaspoons cinnamon to dough. With pastry-brush, frost one layer with melted chocolate. Combine whipped cream with ½ cup chopped almonds. Sandwich layers together with whipped cream, and use chocolate-frosted layer on top. Sprinkle remaining almonds on chocolate frosting. Serve immediately. Makes about 10 servings.

Cream Layer Cake · *Flødelagkage*

For Danish birthdays and other festive occasions.

1 recipe layer cake pastry (either 1, 2, or 3)* baked in 3 10-inch layers
Raspberry jam
2 cups thick vanilla custard*
6 large or 12 small almond macaroons*
1 pint double cream, whipped
Glacé orange and lemon peel or other tinned or glacé fruit
Red currant jelly

Bake layer cake pastry as directed. Place 1 layer of cake on large cake plate. Spread with raspberry jam. Top with one-third of the custard. Place macaroons on custard and top with another third of custard. Top with second layer of pastry, which has been spread with raspberry jam. Top with remaining custard and remaining cake layer. Pipe whipped cream on top and sides of the cake in decorative swirls and rosettes – the Danish cookbook says 'as artistically as you can'. Decorate with fruit and red currant jelly. For birthdays and other festive occasions, decorate further with tiny candles and little paper flags. Makes 10 to 12 servings.

Othello Cake · *Othellokage*

A rich and elegant speciality, which is not nearly as complicated to do as it looks. Bake the pastry in 3 10-inch layers.

1 recipe layer cake pastry 1*, baked in 3 10-inch layers
Chocolate frosting*
2 cups thick vanilla custard*
6 large or 12 small almond macaroons*
16 fl. oz. double cream, whipped

Bake layer cake pastry as directed. Frost 1 layer with chocolate frosting and set aside. Place 1 layer of cake on large cake plate. Spread with one-third of the vanilla custard. Top with macaroons. Spread second third of the vanilla custard on top of macaroons. Top with a layer of pastry. Add a quarter of the whipped cream to remaining custard. Spread this on pastry, but keep it in the middle of the pastry round. Top with remaining pastry layer, frosted side up. Pipe remaining whipped cream around sides of the cake in decorative swirls and rosettes. Makes 10 to 12 servings.

Small Party Cakes · *Smaa Kager*

The following cakes are variations on a theme. Their common base is the dough for layer cake pastry 1, baked in square rather than round layers. After baking, it is then cut into small rounds, squares, fingers, half-moons, or other desired shapes, topped with butter cream* flavoured in different ways, and/or jam, and frosted. In short, these little cakes are the Danish version of *petits fours*.

To make these little cakes, after the pastry has been baked and cut into desired shapes, have all ingredients ready. Place the individual cakes on a cake rack standing on a sheet of waxed paper. Proceed as directed, working quickly.

Don't be disappointed if your first batch does not turn out to be a perfect job. Remember that, with baking too, practice makes perfect.

Rum Tops · *Romtoppe*

1 recipe layer cake pastry 1*
Rum
Butter cream*
White icing*
Maraschino cherries

Cut the pastry into rounds with a pastry cutter or a glass. Add rum to taste to butter cream. Put butter cream into pastry bag and pipe a mound on each pastry round. Chill until stiff. Place icing in pastry tube and cover pastry round and butter cream completely. Decorate each little cake with a Maraschino cherry.

Lemon Tops · *Citrontoppe*

1 recipe layer cake pastry 1*
Butter cream*
Juice and grated rind of 1 lemon
White icing*
Yellow food colouring
Melted sweet cooking chocolate

Proceed as for rum tops,* but combine butter cream with the lemon juice and rind. Add a few drops of yellow food colouring to white icing. Drip chocolate in very thin lines over cake tops.

Raspberry Tops · *Hindbaertoppe*

1 recipe layer cake pastry 1*
Butter cream*
Raspberry jam
White icing*
Red food colouring
Candied violets

Proceed as for rum tops,* but combine butter cream with raspberry jam to taste and colour icing red. Decorate with candied violets.

Mocha Tops · *Moccatoppe*

The same as rum tops,* but with a little instant coffee stirred into the butter cream,* white icing,* and chocolate decoration.

Chocolate Tops

The same as rum tops,* but with a little melted chocolate stirred into the butter cream* and icing. Decorate with walnut halves.

Puff Paste · *Butterdejg*

Puff paste is much used in Denmark, for both sweet and non-sweet dishes. It is made in the same way as in England, and since all good standard English cookbooks have fine recipes for making puff paste, I suggest that you stick by your favourite one for making the base for the following Danish cakes.

I may add that most puff paste confections, such as palm leaves, pretzels, fans, donkey's ears, and other shapes, do not come within the range of Danish home baking but are bought at pastry shops. Since these small cakes are international, I have not included them in this book, limiting myself to typical Danish goodies.

As for the non-sweet uses of puff paste: patty shells, filled with creamed chicken, sweetbreads, mushrooms and other standard fillings, are very popular. Puff paste triangles or half-moons are also served with creamed dishes, or when a note of elegance is wanted for meats, fowl, and game. This, too, falls into the realm of international haute cuisine from France, the cooking that has had enormous influence on Danish cooking.

Prune Tarts · *Svedsketaerte*

This recipe can be made with cooked, chopped, and stoned prunes. But it is infinitely better when made with cooked, stoned, and chopped damsons, in season. The damsons are of varying degrees of tartness and should be sweetened to taste.

Roll out puff paste to ¼-inch thickness. Line a shallow baking-pan with puff paste. Fill (as for a pie) with prepared cooked chopped prunes or damsons. Cut out puff paste in narrow strips. Make a lattice and place on top of fruit. Bake in 425° F., gas mark 7, oven 10 to 15 minutes or until golden brown. Cool. Sprinkle with powdered sugar and decorate with rosettes of whipped cream. Serve immediately.

Cream Puffs and Eclairs · *Vandbakkelser*

These are as popular in Denmark as they are in England. They are also made in exactly the same manner and the recipes can be found in any standard English cookbook.

Linser Cream Tarts · *Fine Linser*

2 cups flour
⅓ cup sugar
½ teaspoon salt
2 egg yolks
1 teaspoon vanilla
6 oz. unsalted butter, cut into pieces
2 cups thick vanilla custard*
16 fl. oz. double cream
½ teaspoon vanilla

Into large bowl or on to baking-board, sift together flour, sugar, and salt. Make a well in the middle. Place egg yolks, vanilla, and sweet butter pieces in the well. With hands, work together until all ingredients are smooth and thoroughly blended. Wrap in waxed paper and chill for 1 hour. Roll out two-thirds of the dough to ⅛-inch thickness, as for pie-crust. Use the dough to line small buttered individual moulds or buttered cupcake or tartlet tins. With floured hands, press dough close to moulds or tins, lining them completely. Trim off excess dough and roll again to ⅛-inch thickness. (If the dough is difficult to handle, chill again; also place individual moulds or tartlet tins in refrigerator while the excess dough is chilling. All the dough must be kept as cold as possible.) As dough is chilling, make vanilla custard, using double cream instead of milk and flavouring with the ½ teaspoon vanilla. Chill filling. Place a little of the filling into each pan lined with dough. Roll out remaining crust. Cover each tart with a piece of rolled-out dough, as for pie. Crimp edges together so that filling won't ooze out, again as when making pie. Bake in a 400° F., gas mark 6, oven about 8 to 10 minutes, or until golden brown. Cool in tins for about 5 minutes. Remove carefully and cool completely before serving.

Chocolate Jelly Roll with Whipped Cream and Strawberries

Chokoladeroulade med Flødeskum og Jordbaer

2 oz. flour
⅓ cup cocoa
1½ teaspoons baking powder
½ teaspoon salt
¼ teaspoon baking soda
3 eggs
3 tablespoons water
1 teaspoon vanilla
6 oz. sugar
Icing sugar
12 fl. oz. double cream, whipped and sweetened to taste
2 cups halved strawberries

Sift together flour, cocoa, baking powder, salt, and baking soda. Combine eggs, water, and vanilla and beat until thick and lemon-coloured. Add sugar gradually, 1 tablespoon at a time, beating thoroughly after each addition. Slowly sift flour mixture into egg mixture and fold in carefully but thoroughly. Grease 15 × 10-inch Swiss roll tin and line with waxed paper. Grease waxed paper in tin. Spread batter evenly in tin. Bake in 350° F., gas mark 4, oven about 30 minutes or until cake tests done. If the dough springs back quickly when the cake is lightly touched with a finger, the cake is done. Sprinkle a kitchen towel heavily with icing sugar. Turn cake on to towel and peel off waxed paper. Trim off crisp edges. Roll warm cake in towel into a roll. Cool on rack, seam side down. Unroll and spread with whipped cream. Place strawberry halves in rows on cream. Re-roll and sprinkle with icing sugar. Refrigerate until serving time.

Mrs Arne Christiansen's Brown Layer Cake with Mocha Filling · *Brun Lagkage med Mocca*

An excellent dessert cake.

Cake

4 oz. butter or margarine
2¼ cups icing sugar
2 eggs
3¼ cups sifted flour
5 dessertspoons cocoa
1½ teaspoons baking soda
1 cup plus 2 tablespoons buttermilk

Filling

4½ oz. butter
1 cup icing sugar
2 egg yolks
1 teaspoon gelatin
2 dessertspoons coffee
1 dessertspoon cocoa
Chocolate frosting*
Almonds

To make *cake*, beat together butter and sugar until fluffy. Add eggs, one at a time, beating well after each addition. Sift together flour, cocoa, and baking soda. Add to egg mixture alternately with buttermilk, beginning and ending with flour mixture. Grease and flour 3 8-inch layer cake tins. Spoon batter into tins and bake in 350° F., gas mark 4, oven about 15 minutes, or until layers test done. Remove layers from tin and cool completely before filling.

To make *filling*, cream together butter and sugar until light. Beat in eggs, one at a time. Soften gelatin in coffee and dissolve over hot water. Stir cocoa into gelatin. Beat gelatin in coffee and dissolve over hot water. Stir cocoa into gelatin. Beat gelatin mixture into egg mixture and blend thoroughly. Chill until thickened and set. Spread mocha filling between layers. Frost top layer and sides with any good chocolate frosting such as the one below and decorate with blanched almonds or walnut halves.

Chocolate Frosting

1⅓ cups sifted icing sugar
¼ teaspoon salt
4 egg yolks
4 dessertspoons milk or cream
2 oz. butter, softened
3 oz. cooking chocolate, melted
1 teaspoon vanilla

Combine all ingredients in bowl. Place bowl over iced water. Beat together until spreading consistency is achieved. Frost cake with decorative swirls.

Meringue Mushrooms · *Marengschampignons*

The Danes love plain and fancy meringues, and shape them in many ways. This is one of the prettiest.

6 egg whites, at room temperature
¼ teaspoon cream of tartar or 2 teaspoons lemon juice
¼ teaspoon salt
1⅔ cups sugar
Finely shaved chocolate

Beat egg whites with salt and cream of tartar or lemon juice until they stand in soft peaks. Beat in sugar gradually, 1 tablespoon at a time, beating until meringue is glossy and stands in stiff peaks. Line a baking-sheet with unglazed paper. Using a pastry bag with a ¾-inch diameter tube, shape half of the meringue (for mushroom stems) into cones that are 2 inches high and measure 1 inch in diameter at the bottom. Make sure that top of cones is a sharp peak. Shape remaining meringue into 1-inch rounds for mushroom caps. Leave a hole in the middle of each cap to fit the top of the stem. Bake in 275° F., gas mark 1, oven about 35 to 45 minutes, or until meringues begin to turn golden. Remove from paper with spatula. Cool thoroughly. Put mushrooms together by fitting stems and caps. If necessary, use a little whipped cream or milk glaze* for glueing. Top with a little finely shaved chocolate. Use as decorations on cakes or cream puddings.

NOTE: *These meringue mushrooms can be made in any desired size. If wanted, they can also be coloured in various shades, using a few drops of food colouring.*

Court Dessert · *Hofdessert*

Easy and elegant, from Ingeborg Suhr's cookbook.

12 meringue shells
6 oz. sweet cooking chocolate
3 dessertspoons cognac or water
1 cup blanched toasted almonds, chopped
16 fl. oz. double cream, whipped

Place 6 meringue shells on large serving-plate. Melt chocolate with cognac or water and stir until smooth. Spread melted chocolate carefully on meringue shells. Sprinkle with chopped almonds. Top with whipped cream. Place remaining 6 shells upside-down on each filled shell to make a ball.

NOTE: *Since meringues look rather bleak on a serving-dish, I would suggest that the serving-plate be decorated with fresh flowers.*

Variation: Instead of meringue shells, use 12 large almond macaroons.* Adjust filling accordingly.

Danish Doughnuts · *Aebleskiver*

A very good home favourite that you never seem to find in a pastry shop or restaurant, which is a great pity. They should be baked in a special tin, but tartlet tins will do.

2 eggs, separated
16 fl. oz. milk, cream, or buttermilk
½ oz. sugar
½ teaspoon salt
¼ teaspoon cardamom
Grated rind of 1 lemon
1 teaspoon baking soda
2 cups sifted plain flour
Melted butter

Beat egg yolks. Gradually beat in milk, cream, or buttermilk, sugar, salt, cardamom, and lemon rind. Sift baking soda into flour. Stir flour into egg mixture. Beat until smooth. Beat egg whites until stiff and fold into batter. Heat a cast-iron tartlet tin *on top of the stove*. Place 2 teaspoons of melted butter into each cup. Rotate pan to coat inside of each cup. Pour batter into cups until half full. Place over low heat and heat until golden brown. Quickly turn, using a knitting needle or an ice pick, and brown other side. Serve very hot with jelly or apple sauce and sprinkled with sugar.

Variation: Before turning doughnut, place 1 thin slice of peeled cooked apple on top of doughnut. Then turn and proceed.

Christmas Cake · *Julekage*

A cake that is pleasant and not as rich as most Christmas cakes.

5 cups sifted plain flour
½ cup potato flour or cornflour
1 teaspoon salt
1 teaspoon cardamom
½ teaspoon cinnamon
½ pint milk
½ oz. dry yeast
4 fl. oz. lukewarm water
6 oz. butter, at room temperature
2 eggs
4 oz. sugar
½ cup raisins
½ cup mixed candied fruit, finely chopped

Sift together first five ingredients. Heat milk to lukewarm. Dissolve yeast in lukewarm water and add to milk. Add softened butter and mix thoroughly. With electric beater, beat together eggs and sugar for 10 minutes. Add to milk mixture. Beat in remaining ingredients. Beat until mixture is smooth and elastic. Cover and let rise in warm place for about 1 hour. Punch down and pour into a greased and floured 10-inch tube pan. Let rise again until dough is 1 inch below the top of the pan. Bake in 350° F., gas mark 4, oven for 40 to 45 minutes, or until golden brown.

Spice Cake · *Astakage*

4 oz. butter
⅞ cup sugar
1 egg
2¼ cups sifted plain flour
1 teaspoon baking soda
1½ teaspoons cardamom
1 dessertspoon cinnamon
1 teaspoon ginger
1½ teaspoons cloves
¼ cup seedless raisins
8 fl. oz. buttermilk

Cream butter until very soft. Gradually beat in sugar, 2 tablespoons at a time. Beat in egg. Sift flour with baking soda and spices. Add raisins to flour. Stir to coat raisins with flour. Add flour mixture and buttermilk to batter alternately, beginning and ending with flour. Spread dough in a well-greased and floured 9-inch square or a 9×5×3-inch loaf tin. Bake in 350° F., gas mark 4, oven for 50 to 55 minutes, or until cake tests done.

Sand Cake · *Sandkage*

One of the most popular cakes, and deservedly so, with a fine, grainy texture and long-keeping qualities. This basic recipe can be varied at will. Ingeborg Suhr, in her classic standard cookbook *Mad* (in Danish, dear reader, this means 'food' pure and simple), recommends flavouring it with vanilla, lemon, orange, chopped glacé peel, chopped almonds, or chopped raisins, etc., depending on one's fancy. I recommend 3 tablespoons cognac or rum.

10 oz. butter
1¼ cups sugar
3 eggs
1 cup sifted plain flour
1 cup cornflour or potato flour
2 teaspoons baking powder
3 dessertspoons cognac or rum

Cream butter until very soft. Gradually beat in sugar, 2 dessertspoons at a time. Beat in eggs, one at a time, beating well after each addition. Sift together flour, cornflour, and baking powder and add to mixture. Beat in cognac or rum. Pour into a well-buttered and floured 8-inch tube pan. Bake in 350° F., gas mark 4, oven about 45 minutes to 1 hour, or until cake tests done. Unmould. Cool, sprinkle with confectioners' sugar, and serve cut in thin slices.

Mazarin Cake · *Mazarinkage*

A cake of Swedish origin, which is also eaten for dessert. It is excellent.

Cake

1⅓ cups sifted plain flour
1 teaspoon baking powder
⅓ cup sugar
4 oz. butter, cut into small pieces
1 egg yolk

Filling

4 oz. butter
2⅔ cups sugar
⅔ cup blanched almonds, very finely ground
½ teaspoon almond flavouring
2 eggs
A few drops green food colouring

To make *cake*, sift together flour, baking powder, and sugar into a large bowl or on baking-board. Make a well in the middle of the flour mixture. Place butter and egg yolk in it. With hands, mix together into a smooth dough. Wrap in waxed paper and chill while preparing filling.

To make *filling*, cream together butter and sugar until thoroughly blended. There should be no graininess from the sugar in the mixture. Add almonds and almond flavouring and blend well. Beat in eggs, one at a time, beating well after each addition. Beat in a few drops of green food colouring to make the mixture a pastel green.

Roll out pastry between 2 sheets of waxed paper to fit the bottom of a 9-inch spring-form pan. Cut remaining dough into a strip 1 inch wide and place it around the inside of the pan, joining it closely to the bottom dough. Or pat dough into deep 9-inch pie pan and crimp edges as when making pie dough. Spread filling on to dough. If there is any pastry left over, roll out thin and place in a lattice over filling. (Both ways are used in making a Mazarin.) Bake in 350° F., gas mark 4, oven about 50 minutes, or until cake tests done. Cool 10 minutes. Remove sides of spring-form pan and let cake cool thoroughly. Place a paper doily on cold cake. Sift icing sugar over doily. Remove doily carefully so as not to disturb sugar pattern. Serve cake preferably the same day. Makes about 10 to 12 servings.

Small Mazarins · *Mazariner*

Proceed as above, but bake in buttered tartlet tins about 15 minutes, or until Mazarins test done.

Almond Pound Cake · *Mandelformkage*

5 oz. butter
1 cup sugar
3 eggs
½ cup blanched almonds, finely ground
½ teaspoon almond flavouring
1⅓ cups sifted plain flour
1 teaspoon baking powder
¼ cup blanched almonds, coarsely chopped

Cream butter until soft and fluffy. Gradually beat in sugar, 1 or 2 tablespoons at a time, beating well after each addition. The mixture should be very thick and white. Beat in eggs, one at a time. Beat at least 3 minutes longer, for a fine texture. Add almonds and almond flavouring and mix thoroughly. Sift together flour and baking powder and add to batter, blending thoroughly. Butter and flour a 9×5×3 inch loaf pan and sprinkle with chopped almonds. Spoon in batter. Bake in 325° F., gas mark 3, oven about 45 to 50 minutes, or until cake tests done.

Almond Paste or Marzipan

Kransekagemasse eller Marcipan

This is practically a Danish staple, so much is it used. There are various ways of making almond paste, and the following recipe has an excellent flavour as well as a smooth, non-grainy texture.

Excellent almond paste imported from Denmark can be bought. But I find that it is so easy to make in a blender that it is worth while to run up a batch and keep it. Covered, almond paste will keep in the refrigerator for several weeks. If it is too stiff to handle, warm the paste in the top of a double boiler over boiling water until it becomes flexible. Almond paste can also be flavoured to taste, with a teaspoon of vanilla, or a tablespoon of cognac or kirsch, and it can be tinted with a few drops of food colouring.

1 cup blanched almonds
1 teaspoon almond flavouring
2 cups sifted icing sugar
2 egg whites, slightly beaten

Grind almonds in electric blender or four times in nut grinder. They must be ground extremely fine. Combine ground almonds, almond flavouring, and icing sugar. Add egg whites, 1 teaspoon at a time, beating vigorously. Knead with hands until paste is absolutely smooth. Makes about 13 oz.

Marzipan Cakes · *Kransekager*

These are perhaps Denmark's best-loved little cakes.

3 lb. almond paste (3½ recipes of almond paste*)
4 to 5 egg whites
2 cups icing sugar
1¼ cups granulated sugar
1 oz. flour
1 teaspoon ammonium carbonate (hartshorn), crushed to powder (see page 165)
White icing*

Heat almond paste in top of double-boiler until soft enough to work. With wooden spoon, blend in egg whites, 1 dessert-spoon at a time. Beat in icing sugar and granulated sugar. Sift flour with ammonium carbonate. Mix or knead until all ingredients are thoroughly blended. Coat hands with icing sugar and keep coated. Roll into strips the thickness of a finger and the length of a baking sheet. Line baking sheet with unglazed brown paper. Grease well and lightly flour brown paper. Place strips on baking-sheet in parallel rows. Pinch each strip with thumb and forefinger with an upward movement so that strips will be broad at the base and slope off to a sharp crease on top. Cut strips into even lengths. Bake in 300° F., gas mark 2, oven about 15 to 20 minutes, or until pale golden. Remove immediately with spatula and cool on a smooth surface. With a pastry tube with a writing tip or with spoon or brush, drip thin strips of icing over cooled cakes in a zigzag pattern.

Marzipan Ring Cake · *Kransekager*

This is the pride of Danish weddings and anniversaries and all occasions when something especially festive is called for. These cakes are seldom made at home but are bought at the pastry shops which specialize in them. Some are 16 and more rings tall.

1 recipe marzipan cakes dough*
White icing*

Proceed as in recipe for marzipan cakes. With hands coated with icing sugar, roll dough into 12 strips about ½ inch thick and 5, 6, 7, 8, 10, 12, 14, 16, 18, 20, 22, and 24 inches in length, respectively. Shape into rings. Bake and ice as above. To assemble, place largest ring on large cake-plate. Spread top with icing. Pile next ring on top of first. Repeat process and end with smallest ring. The icing keeps the rings from slipping. Drip thin strips of white icing over cake rings in a zigzag pattern, as for marzipan cakes.

Marzipan Squares · *Mandelkage*

Roll one recipe marzipan cakes dough* as thinly as possible between two sheets of waxed paper or on a board sprinkled with icing sugar. Bake as in marzipan cake recipe. Make 2, 3, or 4-decker sandwiches by putting layers together with red currant jelly. Cover with whipped cream sweetened to taste and sprinkle with chopped pistachio nuts.

Almond Macaroons · *Makroner*

½ lb. almond paste*
1 cup sifted icing sugar
About 3 egg whites
½ teaspoon almond flavouring
Sugar

Crumble almond paste. Add sugar and work with hands until smooth. Add egg whites, one at a time, mixing well after each addition. Add almond flavouring. Add just enough egg white to make a soft dough that will hold its shape when dropped from a spoon. Line baking-sheets with unglazed brown paper. Pipe mixture through a plain round pastry tube well apart on lined baking-sheets. Or drop from a spoon. Sprinkle with sugar. Let stand at room temperature for about 2 hours. Bake in 300° F., gas mark 2, oven about 20 minutes, or until golden. Place the brown paper sheet with macaroons on a damp cloth and remove macaroons from paper. Cool on rack.

Almond Paste Confections · *Marzipan*

Especially popular at Christmastime. Here are just a few suggestions of the large number of easy home-made almond paste confections. The almond paste can be made from the recipe (see Index), or bought in tins, imported from Denmark. If the paste is too stiff to handle, warm slightly in top of double boiler.

Marzipan Pigs or Mice. Shape marzipan* into small pigs or mice. Dip in melted dipping chocolate (see recipe below). Allow chocolate to harden almost completely but not quite so. Make ears from blanched almond halves, eyes and nose from silver dragées, and tails from coconut strips or glacé orange or lemon peel cut into thin strips. Allow chocolate to harden completely before storing.

Walnuts. Combine equal quantities of marzipan* and chopped walnuts. Roll into small balls and dip in chocolate.

Raspberry Balls. Shape marzipan* into small balls. With the tip of a kitchen knife, make a small hole in each ball. Fill hole with raspberry jam. Seal hole with melted chocolate, using a thin brush. Dip balls in chocolate.*

Rum Cherries. Drain Maraschino cherries and dry between

kitchen towelling. Soak in rum to cover for 24 hours; drain and dry again. Coat cherries with a thin layer of marzipan.* Dip in chocolate.*

How to dip Marzipan Confections in Chocolate

For best results, consult a standard cookbook or a sweet cookbook. But here is an easy way that will work for a few home-made confections.

Use preferably semi-sweet chocolate.

Grate 1 lb. of chocolate finely. Place in top of double-boiler. Melt *extremely* slowly over – not in – hot water. Stir until the chocolate's temperature reaches 130° F. on a sugar thermometer. Remove from heat and cool to about 88° F. Heat water in double-boiler to 90° F. Place top part of double-boiler with chocolate in it.

Have confections to be dipped at room temperature. Dip one piece at a time in melted chocolate, using a steel kitchen fork. Place dipped pieces on cake racks covered with waxed paper. Decorate before coating is completely hardened. Allow confections to harden for at least 5 minutes after decorating before removing them from paper.

DO NOT WORK IN A WARM OR HUMID ROOM. CHOOSE A CRISP DAY FOR DIPPING. KEEP ROOM TEMPERATURE AT ABOUT 60° F. TO 70° F. AND AVOID DRAUGHTS. WORK QUICKLY. REMEMBER, PRACTICE MAKES PERFECT.

Kringle · *Kringle*

This is baked in the shape of a pretzel.

8 fl. oz. milk
¼ oz. dry yeast
¼ teaspoon salt
1 egg
4 oz. butter
4 oz. sugar
4¼ cups sifted plain flour
1 teaspoon ground cardamom
⅓ cup raisins
⅓ cup finely chopped mixed glacé fruit peel
1 egg yolk, beaten
20 almonds, chopped
¼ cup sparkling sugar (bought or made by crushing sugar cubes)

Scald milk and cool to lukewarm (105° to 115° F.). Sprinkle yeast over milk and stir until dissolved. Stir in salt, butter, and sugar. Beat in flour, cardamom, raisins, and glacé fruit peel. Knead well on floured baking board. Place in greased bowl and turn to grease top. Cover; let rise in warm place until double in bulk. Punch down, cover, and let rise again until double in bulk. Punch down. Shape dough into a long 30- to 36-inch roll. The middle of the roll should be about ½-inch thicker than the ends. Place roll on greased and floured cooky sheet and shape into a pretzel. Let rise about 15 minutes. Brush with beaten egg yolk and decorate with chopped almonds. Sprinkle with sugar. Bake in 375° F., gas mark 5, oven about 30 minutes, or until golden brown.

Cones with Whipped Cream

For dessert or afternoon coffee.

2½ oz. butter
2 oz. sugar
2 oz. flour
4 egg whites, stiffly beaten
Whipped cream
Strawberry or other preserves

Melt butter. Stir in sugar and flour. Beat thoroughly. Fold in egg whites. Grease a baking-sheet well and preheat slightly. Drop batter by teaspoonfuls on to it, at least 2 inches apart. With the back of a spoon, flatten dough into long ovals. Bake in 400° F., gas mark 6, oven for 3 to 5 minutes, or until stiff. Loosen carefully with a spatula. Shape while hot into cones. Grease baking-sheet between bakings and bake only a few cookies at one time. Replace baking-sheet in oven if cookies harden too much to roll. Work fast when shaping cones. Cool. Fill with whipped cream and place a little strawberry preserve in the middle of the cream. Or pipe the cream into swirls.

NOTE: *These cones can be made ahead of time. Stored in an air-tight container, they keep well.*

Mrs A. W. Nielsen's Kraemmerhuse Variation: This inspired cook adds 2 teaspoons ground ginger to the batter and mixes the whipped cream with chopped preserved ginger.

Kringler · *Kringler*

These cookies are a little tricky to make since all the ingredients must be kept cold and handled as lightly as possible to make light, crisp cookies. Since they are Danish classics, there are quite a number of ways of making them, but the end result is always about the same: a light, rich, and rather bland cooky.

½ lb. butter
⅔ cup sugar
2 egg yolks
1 teaspoon vanilla or 1 teaspoon cardamom
7–8 oz. sifted plain flour

Cream butter thoroughly. Gradually stir in sugar, 2 tablespoons at a time, mixing well. Add egg yolks, one at a time, beating well after each addition. Beat in vanilla or cardamom. Stir in flour, a little at a time, just enough to make a soft dough that can be piped through a pastry bag. If the dough is too soft, add a little more flour, a dessertspoon at a time. Pipe dough in the shape of pretzels on greased and floured baking-sheets. Preferably, use a fluted tube on the pastry bag. Bake in 350° F., gas mark 4, oven about 8 to 12 minutes, depending on size of kringlers, or until golden brown. Remove from baking-sheets while still warm, using spatula.

Vanilla Wreaths · *Vanillekranse*

¾ lb. butter, at room temperature
1 cup sugar
2 eggs
1½ teaspoons vanilla
4 cups sifted plain flour
½ teaspoon ammonium carbonate (optional)
1 egg white
1 oz. sugar
Candied red cherries, cut in halves

Cream butter with sugar until thoroughly blended. Beat in eggs, one at a time, beating well after each addition. Stir in vanilla. Beat in flour and ammonium carbonate gradually. Chill dough for 2 hours. Break off small pieces and roll with floured hands into 6-inch strips the thickness of a pencil. Shape into rings. For a more artistic effect, twist strips a little before shaping into rings. Place on greased and floured baking-sheets. Beat egg until stiff and beat in sugar. Paint mixture on cookies. Place half a candied cherry on each cooky. Bake in 375° F., gas mark 5, oven about 10 to 12 minutes, or until golden. Remove from sheets while still warm.

Anna Thompsen's Vanilla Rings
Anna Thompsen's Fine Smaakager til Kaffen

Mrs Thompsen, of Guldbjerg in Funen, is the village's star baker.

4 cups plain flour
¾ lb. butter, at room temperature
1 cup sugar
½ cup blanched almonds, finely ground or grated
1 egg
1 teaspoon vanilla

Combine all ingredients. Knead dough until it cleans the side of the bowl. Chill dough for about 30 minutes. Roll dough into rolls ½ inch in diameter. Cut rolls into 4-inch lengths. Shape into rings by bringing ends together. Place close together on greased baking-sheets. Bake in 400° F., gas mark 6, oven for about 8 to 10 minutes, or until golden brown.

Mrs A. W. Nielsen's Finnish Bread · *Finskbrød*

4 oz. butter
2 oz. sugar
1¼ cups sifted plain flour
1 egg yolk, beaten
½ cup blanched almonds, finely chopped

Cream butter and sugar until light and fluffy. Gradually add flour, but mix only until well blended. Do not overbeat. With floured hands, shape dough into 2½ × ½-inch fingers. Dip fingers into beaten egg yolk and roll in almonds. Bake on ungreased baking-sheets in 325° F., gas mark 3, oven for 20 to 25 minutes, or until golden.

Mrs A. W. Nielsen's Horns · *Smørhorn*

9 oz. butter
1 teaspoon dry yeast
1 tablespoon lukewarm (105° to 115° F.) water
2 dessertspoons single cream
1¾ to 2 cups sifted plain flour
Marmalade
Sugar

Cream butter until light and fluffy. Dissolve yeast in lukewarm water. Stir yeast and cream into butter; blend thoroughly. Stir in flour gradually. Drop level dessertspoons of dough on greased baking-sheets. With finger, shape into crescents or rounds, and make a light indentation in the centre of each cooky. Fill hole with marmalade. Sprinkle with sugar. Let stand in a warm place until dough has risen, about 15 minutes. Bake in 325° F., gas mark 3, oven about 20 minutes, or until golden brown.

Sand Tarts · *Sandkager*

6 oz. butter at room temperature
1¼ cups sugar
1 egg
1 egg yolk
1 teaspoon cardamom or other flavouring
2¾ cups sifted plain flour
6 dessertspoons cornflour
2 egg whites
Sugar
Blanched chopped almonds

Beat butter until soft. Gradually beat in sugar, about 2 tablespoons at a time. Beat in egg, egg yolk, cardamom or other flavouring. Sift together flour and cornflour. Add to egg mixture, beating well. Knead dough with hands until smooth. Chill for at least 2 hours. Roll out as thinly as possible on lightly floured board or between two sheets of waxed paper. Cut into small rounds. Paint each round with egg white and sprinkle with sugar and chopped almonds. Bake on greased baking-sheets in 400° F., gas mark 6, oven about 8 minutes, or until golden. Remove from sheets while still warm.

Love Rings · *Kaerlighedskranse*

I suggest adding a little cardamom or another spice, such as mace, to these rich cookies.

8 oz. butter
5 oz. sugar
1 small egg
1 teaspoon mace, cardamom or vanilla
4 hard-boiled egg yolks, sieved
About 12 oz. sifted plain flour

Cream butter and sugar until light. Beat in egg, flavouring, and sieved hard-boiled egg yolks. Stir in flour and blend thoroughly with spoon or with hands to make a smooth dough. Chill dough for at least 2 hours. Roll into 3-inch pencil-thick strips. Place strips on greased and floured baking-sheets and pinch ends together to make rings. Leave 2-inch spaces between rings to allow for expansion during baking. Bake in 325° F., gas mark 3, oven about 10 to 12 minutes, or until golden brown.

Specier · *Specier*

Specie is the old-fashioned Danish word for a *rigsdaler* or dollar in the currency of the times. These round cookies resemble the coin. They are very rich and delicate.

1 lb. butter, at room temperature
1 lb. sugar
3¾ cups sifted plain flour
1 cup chopped blanched almonds

Cream butter until soft. Beat in sugar, 2 tablespoons at a time, beating well after each addition. Add flour and chopped almonds. With hands, work to make a smooth, stiff dough. Shape dough into 2-inch rolls. Wrap in waxed paper and chill overnight in refrigerator. With sharp knife, slice very thinly. Place cookies on ungreased baking-sheets. Bake in 350° F., gas mark 4, oven about 10 minutes, or until golden brown.

Currant Cookies · *Korendekager*

½ cup currants
8 oz. butter
1 cup sugar
3 eggs
Grated rind of 1 lemon
1 dessertspoon cognac (optional)
2½ cups flour
½ teaspoon powdered ammonium carbonate or baking powder

Scald currants with hot water and dry between folds of a kitchen towel. Cream butter and sugar until light. Beat in eggs, one at a time, beating well after each addition. Stir in lemon rind and cognac. Sift together flour and baking powder. Gradually beat into egg mixture. Drop from teaspoon on to greased and floured baking-sheets. Sprinkle a few currants on each cooky and press down with wet spoon. Bake in 375° F., gas mark 5, oven for 8 to 10 minutes, or until golden brown.

NOTE: *A crisper cooky is made by using 2 cups flour and ½ cup cornflour instead of 2½ cups flour.*

Medals · *Medaljer*

1 recipe dough for linser cream tarts*
2 cups vanilla custard, made with double cream instead of milk
Milk glaze*
Red currant jelly

Roll dough very thin. Cut into rounds. Bake on greased baking-sheets in 350° F., gas mark 4, oven about 7 minutes, or until golden brown. Cool thoroughly. Spread half the number of rounds with a little vanilla filling, placing the filling in the middle of the cooky. Top with remaining cookies sandwich fashion. Frost with milk glaze. At serving time place a dab of red currant jelly in the centre of each cooky.

Mrs Peter Heering's Klejner · *Klejner*

Another traditional Christmas cooky. This one comes from the wife of the head of the Cherry Heering Company, who lives in the most beautiful old house and knows a great deal about fine food.

4 eggs
1 cup sugar
2 dessertspoons double cream
4½ oz. butter, softened
1 lb. plain flour
2 fl. oz. cognac
Deep fat for frying
Icing sugar

Beat eggs together with sugar until thick. Beat in cream, butter, flour, and cognac, beating well after each addition. Let dough stand in cool place for about 1 hour. On lightly floured board, roll out to ½-inch thickness. Cut into 1¼-inch wide strips with a pastry-cutter. Cut these strips into 4-inch pieces. With the point of a sharp knife, slash the middle of each strip. Pull one end of the strip through the slash to make a half-bow. Fry in deep fat for 2 to 3 minutes. Drain on absorbent paper. Sprinkle with icing sugar.

Mrs Peter Heering's Brown Cakes · *Brune Kager*

An excellent recipe for a favourite Christmas cooky.

1⅓ cups (1 lb.) treacle
1 cup sugar
1 dessertspoon cloves
1 teaspoon ginger
8 oz. butter
4 cups sifted plain flour
½ teaspoon bicarbonate of soda
3½ tablespoons water
Grated rind of 2 lemons
¼ cup finely chopped candied peel
½ lb. blanched almonds, ground
½ teaspoon almond extract
Blanched almond halves

Heat treacle and add sugar, cloves, and ginger. In large bowl, cut butter into flour until mixture resembles a fine meal. Dissolve baking soda in water. Add sugar mixture and soda mixture to flour. Stir to mix and blend thoroughly. Add lemon rind, candied peel, blanched almonds, and almond extract. Knead dough with hands. Let stand at room temperature for 2 days. Roll out thinly on floured board. Cut into rounds with a cooky cutter or a glass and place half a blanched almond in the centre of each cooky. Bake on greased baking-sheets in 375° F., gas mark 5, oven for about 8 to 10 minutes.

Mrs Rasmussen's Brown Cookies · *Brune Kager*

An excellent version of the classic, from Guldbjerg on Funen.

2 cups treacle
1 cup brown sugar
4 oz. butter
1 cup unblanched chopped almonds
1 teaspoon cinnamon
½ teaspoon ginger
½ teaspoon cloves
1 teaspoon of bicarbonate of soda
Grated rind of 1 orange
6 cups sifted plain flour
1 egg white, slightly beaten
Blanched almond halves
Bits of candied orange or lemon peel

Combine treacle, brown sugar, and butter. Bring to the boil. Remove from heat. Add almonds, spices and bicarbonate of soda. Stir in orange peel and flour. Beat until smooth. Cover with a towel and let dough stand at room temperature for 3 days. Knead on lightly floured baking-board until smooth. Roll to ⅛-inch thickness and cut into rounds or oblongs. Place on greased and floured baking-sheets. Brush with beaten egg white. Decorate each cooky with half an almond or a bit of candied peel. Bake in 375° F., gas mark 5, oven for 10 to 12 minutes, or until firm and crisp.

Peppernuts · *Pebernødder*

1 cup sugar
5 dessertspoons water
2½ tablespoons treacle
2 teaspoons cinnamon
1 teaspoon cloves
1½ teaspoons ginger
4 oz. butter or margarine
1½ teaspoons baking soda
3 dessertspoons cognac
3 to 4 cups plain flour

Combine sugar, water, treacle, cinnamon, cloves, and ginger and heat through but do not let boil. Remove from heat and stir in butter or margarine. Stir until mixture is cool. Add baking soda, cognac, and enough flour to make a stiff dough. Let dough stand at room temperature for 36 to 48 hours. Knead again. Roll out as thinly as possible and cut into Christmas shapes. Or snip off small pieces of dough, the size of a walnut, and roll into balls. Bake on greased baking-sheets in 375° F., gas mark 5, oven about 10 minutes.

Butter Cream for Small Cakes · *Smørcreme*

4 oz. butter
4 oz. white cooking fat (like Spry)
1¼ cups sifted icing sugar
2 large or 3 small eggs
1½ teaspoons vanilla

Cream butter and fat until well blended. Beat in sugar 1 tablespoon at a time, beating well after each addition. Beat in eggs, one at a time. Beat in vanilla. Beat 5 minutes longer. Makes about 1½ cups.

Thick Vanilla Custard or Filling · *Vanillecreme*

For Danish pastries, layer cakes, etc.

12 fl. oz. milk or single cream
1 vanilla bean
4 oz. sugar
1 oz. flour
4 egg yolks, well beaten

Scald milk or single cream with vanilla bean. In top of double boiler, combine sugar, flour, and egg yolks. Remove vanilla bean from scalded milk. Gradually stir milk into egg mixture. Blend thoroughly. Cook over hot (not boiling) water, stirring constantly, until just boiling. Remove from heat immediately. Stir until cooled to prevent top from crusting. Cool thoroughly before using. Makes about 1¾ cups.

White Icing · *Aeggehvideglasur*

2 egg whites
2 to 2½ cups sifted icing sugar
Juice of 1 lemon

Beat egg whites until stiff. Beat in icing sugar and lemon juice until stiff and of correct spreading consistency. Makes about 1½ cups.

Milk Glaze · *Maelkeglasur*

For *medaljer** and other cookies.

1 cup icing sugar
1 dessertspoon hot milk
½ teaspoon vanilla

Sift icing sugar. Stir in hot milk and vanilla and stir until smooth and of spreading consistency. Makes about 1 cup.

Thin Water, Orange, Lemon, Brandy, or Rum Icing · *Glasur*

This is the basic recipe, to be increased as needed.

About 1½ cups sifted icing sugar
About 2 dessertspoons water or orange or lemon juice, brandy or rum or any other liquid flavouring

Sift icing sugar into a bowl. Gradually stir in flavouring, beating vigorously to make a smooth paste. Add more sugar, if necessary, to make desired spreading consistency, but only very little, about ½ teaspoon at a time. Makes about 1½ cups.

Chef G. L. Wennberg's Danish Pastry and Other Cakes

Danish Pastry Basic Recipe
Cream Buns
Carnival Buns
Spandauers
Triangles
Scrubbing Brushes and Combs
Pastry Filling for Danish Pastries
Chef Wennberg's Orange Meringues
  Meringues
  Orange Mousse
  Fondant Icing
Princess Margrethe's Almond Garland
  Cake
  Chocolate Glaze
  Fruit Salad
  Half-frozen Custard Sauce
Chef Wennberg's Superlative Chocolate Orange Cake
  Cake
  Chocolate Coating
  Marzipan Coating
King Frederik's 50th Birthday Cake
  Cake
  Vanilla Custard Filling
  Butter Cream Frosting
  Book Cover
  Decorators' Icing

About Chef G. L. Wennberg's Recipes

The following recipes were given me by the most famous pastry chef in Denmark, if not in all of Scandinavia. The late Chef G. L. Wennberg, a tall, kindly man of Swedish descent, was the pastry chef at the Hotel d'Angleterre in Copenhagen. The excellence and beauty of his work had to be seen to be believed; it was in the tradition of such great dessert cooks of the eighteenth and nineteenth centuries as Carême.

Chef Wennberg was kind enough to give me these recipes prior to publication in his own book and I have adapted them for the home cook to keep the taste and appearance of the originals as much as possible.

Chef G. L. Wennberg's Danish Pastry . *Wienerbrød*

There are any number of recipes for Danish pastry, the glory of Danish baking. I have chosen Chef Wennberg's version because his *wienerbrød* is superlatively light and flaky. Imported Danish butter should be used.

If any of my readers should not turn out to be a perfect baker of Danish pastries, he or she should take heart. In Denmark, these *wienerbrød* are almost invariably bought at a bakery that specializes in them, and they all seem to do just this.

Before embarking on the recipe, I suggest reading the following observations made by Chef G. L. Wennberg. I've tried to keep them as much as possible in his own language.

It is important to make sure that the dough and the butter are the same temperature and of the same consistency. If the butter is too hard in comparison with the dough the resulting pastry will be uneven and lumpy. The butter should not be too soft as it then breaks through the dough on being rolled, thus spoiling the layers.

A really delicious and attractive piece of Danish pastry is a true delight and can be achieved only by the confectioner or baker who has sufficient interest and fondness for his trade. It is also important to take care over forming the pastry, to allow it to rise properly and to see to it that it is baked right away. Danish pastry should never be allowed to rise in a very moist atmosphere, or in too dry heat, but should be left to rise slowly in a warm, slightly moist place. If the dough is left to rise in an overheated room, the butter will melt out of the dough and if left to rise in too dry a heat the dough will form a crust. The length of time that the dough should be left to rise varies in accordance with the kind of Danish pastry to be produced. Danish pastry should always be put into a very hot oven and then baked slowly at a more moderate temperature. Danish pastry tastes best fresh from the oven.

Danish Pastry Basic Recipe

Wienerbrød à la Wennberg

½ oz. dry yeast
2 fl. oz. lukewarm water
6 fl. oz. milk
1 oz. sugar
1 egg
1 egg yolk
¼ teaspoon salt
1 teaspoon cardamom
1 lb. unsalted butter or unsalted margarine (use 3 oz. to prepare the dough)
1 lb. sifted plain flour

Dissolve yeast in lukewarm water. Stir until completely dissolved. Heat milk to lukewarm. Beat in sugar, egg, egg yolk, salt, cardamom, and 3 oz. of the butter or margarine. Stir in dissolved yeast. Beat in flour. Turn dough out on a floured board and knead until smooth, soft, and pliable. Cover dough and allow it to rise until doubled in bulk. Punch down and roll dough into a 12 × 12-inch square. Work remaining butter or margarine under iced water until soft and pliable. Knead until all the water has oozed out. Shape the butter into a square and place it on the dough. Working quickly, pat the butter with the finger-tips so that the entire surface of the dough is covered with butter. Cover dough with sheet of waxed paper. With a cold rolling-pin (chill it in the refrigerator) roll out dough into an oblong shape. The dough should be about ½-inch thick or thinner. Remove waxed paper. Fold the sheet of dough into thirds. Chill in the refrigerator for 10 minutes. Repeat the rolling, folding, and chilling process twice more. Roll out again to a ½-inch thick oblong, but fold in half. Chill in the refrigerator for 30 minutes. (Dough should be rolled, folded, and chilled 4 times altogether.) Line baking-sheets with foil and turn up edges. (This is to prevent butter from oozing into oven during baking.) Shape pastries and place at least 3 inches apart on foil-lined sheets. Preheat oven to 400° F., gas mark 6, and lower temperature to 350° F., gas mark 4, when pastries are placed in oven.

Cream Buns · *Cremeboller*

1 recipe Danish pastry*
Thick vanilla custard*
Beaten egg yolk

Roll out chilled dough to $\frac{1}{3}$-inch thickness. Cut dough into 4-inch squares. Place a spoonful (the size of a walnut) of thick vanilla custard in the centre of each square. Fold the four corners around the custard. Place on foil-lined baking sheet with folds facing downwards. Press lightly on top and brush with beaten egg yolk. Allow to rise for 15 minutes. While pastries are rising, preheat oven to 400° F., gas mark 6. Lower temperature to 350° F., gas mark 4, when placing pastries in the oven. Bake for 15 to 20 minutes, or until golden brown.

Carnival Buns · *Fastelavnsboller*

1 recipe Danish pastry*
Raisins
Chopped candied mixed peel
Beaten egg yolk
Thin water icing*

Roll out chilled dough to $\frac{1}{3}$-inch thickness. Cut dough into 4-inch squares. Place a few raisins and a little chopped candied peel in the centre of each square. Fold the 4 corners around fruit. Proceed as for cream buns,* but ice the carnival buns with a little thin water icing while still warm.

Spandauers · *Spandauer*

1 recipe Danish pastry*
Raspberry jam
Beaten egg yolk

Proceed as for cream buns,* but use raspberry jam for filling instead of vanilla custard.

Triangles · *Trekanter*

1 recipe Danish pastry*
Pastry filling*
Beaten egg yolk
Chopped walnuts or almonds
Thin water icing*

Roll out chilled dough to $\frac{1}{3}$-inch thickness. Cut into 4-inch squares. Place 1 heaped teaspoon pastry filling in the centre of each square. Fold over to form a triangle. Press edges together, sealing in filling. Slash edges with a sharp knife 5 to 6 times. Place on foil-lined baking-sheets. Brush pastries with beaten egg yolk and sprinkle with chopped nuts. Allow to rise for 15 minutes. While pastries are rising, preheat oven to 400° F., gas mark 6. Lower temperature to 350° F., gas mark 4, when placing pastries in the oven. Bake for 15 to 20 minutes, or until golden brown. Top with a little thin water-icing while still warm.

Scrubbing Brushes and Combs · *Skrubber og Kamme*

The first steps for making these two differently shaped Danish pastries are similar.

1 recipe Danish pastry*
Pastry filling*
Beaten egg yolk
Sugar
Finely chopped walnuts or almonds

Roll chilled dough into a rectangle measuring 20 × 6 inches. Cut the dough lengthwise into two strips. Spread a pencil-thick strip of pastry filling down the centre of the two strips of dough. Fold one third of the dough lengthwise over the filling. Brush dough with beaten egg yolk. Fold other side over the first. You should now have a long three-layered strip of dough. Press down lightly. Turn upside down and brush smooth side with beaten egg yolk. Combine granulated sugar and nuts.

To shape scrubbing brushes, cut strip of dough into 12 pieces, making diagonal cuts. Dip pieces in sugar-nut mixture and place on foil-lined baking-sheets. Allow to rise 15 minutes. While pastries are rising, preheat oven to 400° F., gas mark 6. Lower temperature to 350° F., gas mark 4, when placing pastries in the oven. Bake for 15 to 20 minutes, or until golden brown.

To shape combs, cut strip of dough into 12 pieces, making straight cuts. With a sharp knife, gash one side of each piece 4 or 5 times, cutting evenly towards the filling, but without touching the filling. Dip pieces in sugar-nut mixture and proceed as above.

Pastry Filling for Danish Pastries · *Remonce*

4 oz. butter
4 oz. sugar
1½ teaspoons vanilla

Cream butter and sugar until light and fluffy. Stir in vanilla. Use for Danish pastries.*

Chef Wennberg's Orange Meringues

Another of the chef's spectacular desserts. In spite of the long recipe, it is not difficult to make. The meringue shells and the filling can be prepared in advance, but they must be assembled and glazed just before serving.

Meringues

5 egg whites, at room temperature
1⅔ cups sugar
2 teaspoons grated orange rind
Sifted icing sugar

Orange Mousse

¾ cup sugar
4 fl. oz. fresh orange juice
4 egg yolks
2 teaspoons grated orange rind
16 fl. oz. double cream

Fondant Icing

1½ cups sugar
6 fl. oz. water
1½ dessertspoons golden syrup
6½ cups sifted icing sugar
1 dessertspoon grated orange rind
Yellow food colouring
2 oz. sweet chocolate, melted

To make meringues: Beat egg whites until stiff. Beat in sugar, 1 tablespoon at a time, until mixture is very stiff. Fold in grated orange rind. Line baking-sheets with ordinary unglazed brown paper. With a spoon or a pastry bag shape meringue into mounds resembling half an orange. Sprinkle meringues with icing sugar. Bake in 275° F., gas mark 1, oven about 40 minutes, or until meringues are crusty. Remove meringues from brown paper. Turn upside-down and hollow out carefully with a teaspoon. Take care not to break shell. Store in airtight container until ready to use.

To prepare *orange mousse:* Over medium heat, boil sugar and orange juice for 5 minutes. Beat egg yolks in top of double boiler until very thick. Gradually beat in orange syrup. Beat over hot (not boiling) water until smooth and thick. Fold in grated orange rind. Remove from hot water and beat until cool. Whip cream and fold into cooled orange custard. Pour mixture into a freezing tray and freeze until firm. Stir several times during freezing process to prevent iciness.

To prepare *fondant icing:* Combine sugar, water, and golden syrup. Bring mixture to the boil and cook until clear. Remove from heat and cool for 5 minutes. Gradually beat in icing sugar and grated orange rind. Beat until smooth and lukewarm. Keep over hot (not boiling) water. Colour with yellow food colouring until a bright orange.

To assemble *orange meringues:* Fill meringue shells with orange mousse and press 2 shells together to form one orange. Place filled meringues on wire rack over waxed paper and spoon entire surface with fondant icing. Let icing harden. With a thin brush, dot the top of the orange meringue with a little melted chocolate to resemble the stem of an orange. Serve immediately. Makes about 12 orange meringues.

NOTE: *Left-over icing can be cooled and reheated for new use. It may then be necessary to add a few drops of water in order to thin it for spreading consistency.*

Princess Margrethe's Almond Garland

Chef Wennberg created this elegant dessert cake in honour of the then Heir to the Throne of Denmark, now Queen Margrethe. The blanched almonds must be ground extremely fine and I advise the use of an electric blender. Next best to a blender is a nut grinder – the nuts must be ground 4 times. On no account use a meat grinder because nuts ground in a meat grinder are apt to be oily.

Cake

2½ cups finely ground blanched almonds
2 egg whites
¾ cup sugar
3 tablespoons Cherry Heering
8 egg whites
Chocolate glaze
Fruit salad
Spun sugar (optional)
Fresh strawberries, unhulled
Curaçao
Sugar
Blanched almonds
Half-frozen custard sauce

Combine almonds with the 2 egg whites and sugar in a small saucepan. Heat mixture to lukewarm over low flame, stirring constantly. Remove from heat and stir in Cherry Heering. Cool. Beat the 8 egg whites until they stand in stiff peaks. Fold egg whites into almond mixture. Grease a 9-inch ring mould. Pour mixture into ring mould. Place in a pan of water, allowing the water to reach half-way up the mould. Bake in 350° F., gas mark 4, oven for 30 to 35 minutes. Remove ring mould from water and cool on rack for 10 minutes. Unmould carefully on large serving platter, preferably silver. When almond ring is thoroughly cooled, frost completely with chocolate glaze. Fill the centre of the ring with fruit salad. Top the ring with a crown made of spun sugar. (For spun sugar recipe, consult standard or sweet cookbook.) Sprinkle unhulled strawberries with curaçao and dip in sugar. Place strawberries around the ring alternately with blanched almonds. Serve with half-frozen custard sauce.

Chocolate Glaze

1½ oz. unsweetened chocolate
1½ oz. unsalted butter, melted
3 dessertspoons rum
1½ cups sifted icing sugar
½ cup chopped walnuts
½ cup chopped pistachio nuts

Melt chocolate over hot water. Add butter and stir until butter is melted. Add rum and icing sugar. Beat mixture until smooth. While warm spread quickly over the almond garland* ring. Sprinkle chopped walnuts and pistachios over chocolate glaze.

Fruit Salad

The idea is to have a colourful combination of fruits. About 2 to 3 cups of fruit salad are needed. Combine orange sections, (free of white membrane), apricots, peaches, strawberries, or any other suitable fruit. Sprinkle fruit with a little lemon juice to prevent discolouring and flavour with curaçao. Chill for 1 hour. Drain fruit before filling centre of the ring with it.

Half-frozen Custard Sauce

Freeze vanilla custard filling* until mushy. Beat twice during freezing process to avoid graininess.

Chef Wennberg's Superlative Chocolate Orange Cake

This cake is different from our chocolate cakes; it is drier and fragrant with orange. The keeping qualities are excellent. It is also easy to make.

Cake

2¾ cups flour
¾ cup cocoa
3 teaspoons baking powder
Grated rind from 4 large oranges
1 lb. unsalted butter
1¾ cups sugar
4 eggs
6 fl. oz. lukewarm water
6 fl. oz. milk

Chocolate Coating

3 4-oz. bars sweet cooking chocolate

Marzipan Coating

2 cups almond paste*
Green food colouring

To make *cake*, sift flour with cocoa and baking powder. Stir in orange rind. Cream butter until soft. Gradually beat in sugar, 2 dessertspoons at a time, beating well after each addition. Beat in eggs, one at a time, beating well. Combine water and milk. Alternately add flour mixture and milk to the batter, beginning and ending with flour. Pour into greased and floured 13 × 4-inch baking-pan. Bake in 350° F., gas mark 4, oven about 1 hour, or until cake tests done. Let stand at room temperature for about 5 minutes before unmoulding. When thoroughly cooled, frost with chocolate coating and with marzipan coating. Decorate cake with candied violets, roses, and mimosa.

To make *chocolate coating*, melt chocolate over (not in) hot water. Stir until very smooth. Spread with a pastry brush over cooled cake. Smooth with a warmed spatula or knife. Coating must be very smooth. Chill until firm.

To make *marzipan coating:* If almond paste is too stiff to handle, warm slightly in top of double-boiler. Work in sufficient green food colouring for desired shade. Between 2 sheets of waxed paper, roll out almond paste to ¼-inch thickness or thinner. Roll it long and wide enough to cover the top and sides of the cake. Remove 1 sheet of waxed paper. Flip almond paste on to cake and remove the second sheet of wax paper. Trim edges of marzipan to fit around cake. Cake must be completely covered with almond paste. Use remaining almond paste to decorate cake with hearts, bows, or any desired shapes. Finally, decorate cake with candied flowers.

King Frederik's 50th Birthday Cake

Chef Wennberg made this cake for King Frederik IX, the late King of Denmark. The original cake was exquisitely decorated with a picture of Amalienborg, the royal residence, executed in cocoa, and decorative crowns, initials, and dates were piped on to the cake with gilt icing.

The cake is in the shape of an ancient book, and according to English standards, it is not a cake proper but a confection of almond paste and fillings. Only a skilled confectioner could reproduce the magnificent decorations, and I have therefore omitted the picture of Amalienborg and other details from the recipe that follows. However, a very creditable replica of the original will be achieved – a truly magnificent confection.

I must warn my readers that this is *not* a cake for beginners. The almond paste can be home-made or bought imported from Denmark.

Cake Layers

6 cups almond paste*
About 4 fl. oz. cognac
4 fl. oz. Cherry Heering

Vanilla Custard Filling

16 fl. oz. single cream
2 oz. butter
2½ oz. flour
5 oz. sugar
½ teaspoon salt
8 fl. oz. cold single cream
4 egg yolks, well beaten
2 teaspoons vanilla

Butter Cream Frosting

4 oz. butter
About 1 lb. sifted icing sugar
2 egg yolks
1½ dessertspoons cognac

Book Cover

4½ cups almond paste*
Cocoa
Yellow food colouring

Decorators' Icing

2½ cups sifted icing sugar
¼ cup egg whites
Yellow food colouring

To make *cake layers*: Divide almond paste into 4 pieces. Roll out each piece between two sheets of waxed paper to ⅛-inch thickness and into a sheet measuring 8 × 10 inches. There should be four 8 × 10-inch sheets. Line baking-sheets with ordinary unglazed brown paper. Lightly grease brown paper. Remove top piece of waxed paper from almond paste sheets. Flip sheet of almond paste uncovered side down on to baking-sheet. Peel off remaining piece of waxed paper. Repeat until all four sheets of almond paste are on baking-sheets. Bake in 300° F., gas mark 2, oven for 15 to 20 minutes or until deep brown, puffed and dry to the touch. Remove from oven. Cool to lukewarm. Flip sheets of almond paste carefully onto a rack. Remove brown paper carefully. Cool layers. Sprinkle 2 layers with cognac and 2 with Cherry Heering.

To make *vanilla custard filling:* Combine cream and butter and heat until butter is melted. Combine flour, sugar, salt, and cold cream. Stir until smooth. Gradually stir into hot cream. Cook over low heat, stirring constantly, until smooth and thick. Beat egg yolks. Add some of the hot mixture to egg yolks. Blend well. Add egg mixture to the hot mixture. Cook, stirring constantly, for another 5 minutes. Cook slightly and stir in vanilla. Do not chill. Place one sheet of baked almond paste on a large serving-platter. Cover with one third of the vanilla custard. Repeat, using all four layers of almond paste, ending with almond paste. Cool. Trim cake to make all four edges even.

To make *butter cream frosting:* Cream butter until fluffy. Gradually beat in half of the icing sugar. Beat in egg yolks. Gradually beat in cognac. Beat in remaining sugar gradually until frosting can be spread easily.

To prepare *book cover:* Take 2¼ cups of the almond paste and work cocoa into it to make a medium mahogany-brown colour. Take ⅔ cup of the remaining white almond paste and tint it with yellow food colouring to a golden colour. Take remaining white almond paste and roll it to ¼-inch thickness. Cut it into long strips to fit and cover one 10-inch and two 8-inch sides of the cake. Before placing the strips on the side of the cake, mark the strips in grooves lengthwise with the back of a knife to resemble the pages of a book. Take 1 cup of the brown almond paste and roll it to ¼-inch thickness. Cut it into a strip to fit and cover the other 10-inch side of the cake. This represents the spine of the book and should be marked accordingly. Take ½ cup of the brown almond paste and again roll it to ¼-inch thickness. Cut this into a 4 × 6-inch oblong and into two triangles of the same size. Reserve. The oblong will bear the inscription of the cake and the triangles will represent the corners of the book. Take the remaining brown, yellow, and white almond paste and knead it together until a marbled colour is achieved. Roll out to ¼-inch thickness. Trim to the same length and width as the cake. This is the cover of the book. Place it accordingly on the top of the cake. Now place the brown oblong at the centre of the top of the cake, on the marbled cover. Place the triangles on the upper and lower corners of the cake. The 'book' is now made and ready for decorating with decorators' icing.

To make *decorators' icing:* Combine icing sugar and egg whites and beat with an electric beater until icing holds its shape. Tint with yellow food colouring to a golden colour. Decorate the oblong in the centre, using the writing tip of a pastry tube, with a crown and the initials of H.M. the late King Frederik IX and H.M. Queen Ingrid, the Queen Mother, if this is to be a Danish cake; or, to be up to date, write H.M. Queen Margrethe on the cake. Decorate spine accordingly.

NOTE: *Of course, the cake may be decorated with any other designs or initials.*

How to Serve Food in the Danish Manner

It's a great pleasure to sit down to a Danish meal, and this pleasure is one that can be duplicated in England. When you start setting your table, think of it as a beautiful picture, in which all elements harmonize. The cloth may be damask, cotton, or linen, block printed, hand-woven or hand-embroidered. The Danes also use mats in an interesting manner; mats or runners are placed parallel on the table: the bare wood between them holds the flower arrangements and the candles. The candles are tall and slender, set in low sconces of wrought iron, crystal, or silver. The candles are usually placed at regular intervals along the table, among the flower or fruit arrangements. The flowers are always most beautifully arranged, with much imagination. There might be a low row of nosegays, and small matching ones tucked into the napkins, or mixed blossoms lined by smilax and fern, or strands of ivy and flowers winding around the candles. Table decorations include figurines, usually made by china manufacturers such as the famous Copenhagen Porcelain Manufactory, or Bing & Grøndahl, or the Denmark or others. The figurines are as varied as the hostess's taste, and suited to the occasion. Chickens may march along the table for an Easter dinner, under an Easter egg tree with decorated eggs hanging from bare branches, or an army of tin soldiers will please a little boy at his birthday party.

Danish hostesses, like English ones, have to be their own cooks and waitresses. In order to make serving easier, and to have plenty of room for the serving-dishes, both ends of the dining-table are left free for this purpose. Or the flowers may stand at one end of the table and the food at the other.

Danish china, it seems redundant to say, is beautiful. The pattern most frequently seen is the blue and white one made by the Copenhagen Porcelain Manufactory; it is their pattern No. 1. It makes all foods look utterly fresh, and that's why you see it everywhere in Denmark, in homes, restaurants, and on shipboard.

When you set your table in the Danish manner, fold the napkins as artfully as you know how to. In Denmark, napkin folding is an art taught to home economics students and shown in standard cookbooks with photographs and diagrams. Danish napkins are folded into fleurs-de-lis, Viking ships, umbrellas, palm leaves and bishops' mitres, to mention just a few folds. For family use, napkins are kept in individual rings, paper napkins being still the exception rather than the rule.

Next to the silver. Denmark is the land of fine silver, both traditional and modern. Silver designers are known by their names as we know TV artists. The traditional silver of Georg Jensen is perhaps the best known. He was a great artist who made Danish silver famous all over the world. Other fine silver designers are Cohr, Hans Hansen, Frantz Hingelberg, and A. Michelsen. Beautiful silver is also designed by artists in other fields. Magnus Stephenson, an architect, is one of them, and no one has ever designed casseroles, ice buckets, and table settings of a purer and more exquisite line.

Danish silver is not inexpensive, even in Denmark, and the Danes often buy the beautiful stainless steel table settings, which are often designed by the same artists as design the silver. On a Danish table, the silver is set as in England. The glasses, too, are set like ours, but there won't be one for water.

Denmark also makes some of the beautiful modern table and kitchen accessories. The casseroles, wooden boards, in fact all the products of Dansk Designs, are outstanding.

One of the most admirable Danish customs is to serve hot foods hot on heated plates, and to keep them hot on candle and other warmers. This is standard practice.

Soup is served from a tureen, right at the table, which looks hospitable and, besides, keeps the soup hot.

The meat dish is served very differently from ours. The Danes don't carve meat at the table or at the sideboard; this is done in the kitchen. The carved meat slices are dished up on a big, handsome platter and surrounded by vegetables arranged in a decorative manner. A platter of roast pork will hold the meat slices along one side, bundles of string beans at one end, browned potatoes at the other and, in between, grilled mushroom caps and tomato slices. A chicken platter will have the meat piled in the middle and a large bundle of asparagus at one end and baked tomato shells filled with green peas and topped with grilled mushroom caps at the other.

All the food, whatever comes to the table, is decorated with lettuce leaves, parsley or dill sprigs, radish roses, and tomato slices, arranged with an eye for shape and colour. Desserts are glorious baroque creations, almost too beautiful to eat.

The Danes don't go in for buffet parties or for tea or coffee parties where you balance your cups and plates. The table is set for sitting down, and the idea is to make the guest comfortable and cosy.

Finally, if you really want to do as the Danes do, decorate your table and your food with flags. How the Danes feel about their flag is best described by a Dane, Willy Breinholst.

The flag is run up on the slightest excuse. It is hoisted if there is a birthday in your family, it is hoisted if there is a birthday in the family next door, it is hoisted when you are expecting guests . . . when they leave . . . on holidays, on Sundays, or simply because everybody else has hoisted theirs. On bigger festive occasions, such as weddings and the like, one flag is not enough. You decorate the whole house with flags, flags are hung outside the door, in the windows, on the walls, on the table, and on the cake. On the King's birthday or other days of celebration among the royal family you go about with a flag in your hand, a flag in your buttonhole, and a flag in your hat.

Danish Hospitality

The Danes are a hospitable people, among themselves and to foreigners, but their hospitality is on the formal side until real friendship has set in.

A Danish invitation means an abundance of glorious food, gloriously presented. You can't tell a Danish hostess that you'd just as soon have only a cup of coffee, if you must have anything at all. A groaning board is expected among the Danes, and a groaning board the guests will have – and enjoy. A Danish hostess is used to persuading her guests who are waiting to be persuaded to have a little something, even though the guests say they have just had coffee at home. After many 'I couldn'ts' and 'Really, you must try just a little piece', everybody sits down and tucks away the cakes and cookies that a wise Danish hostess bakes in advance for just such an occasion. After this, the guests compliment the hostess and ask for her recipes, which she is happy to share.

In Denmark, you may be invited for lunch, for coffee, for dinner, or for after dinner. Towards midnight, when you're thinking of going home, your hostess will urge you to stay, because *natmad* (night food) is about to be served. This will be smørrebrød, simple or elaborate, with a bottle of Carlsberg or Tuborg beer. When the party goes on, tea and cookies may be produced. This is done to postpone the good-byes, for a Danish dinner party is judged not only on the amounts and the quality of the food but also on the lateness of the hour at which the guests leave.

It is customary to take flowers with you the first time you go to somebody's house, and it is very nice if you do so any time you go. Better still, send the flowers beforehand so that your hostess will have a chance to show her art at displaying them to the best advantage. The Danes are the greatest flower lovers on earth; the most beautiful flowers grow in profusion in houses and public gardens, and they make you drool, as you suppress your thieving instincts.

When you receive an invitation in Denmark, or when you have a date with a Dane, you *must* be punctual. This is to be interpreted literally, to the minute. There is no before-dinner drinking, except for a little sherry, drunk quickly, and a six o'clock invitation means that you're going to eat at a quarter past six. Not bringing flowers on your visit may be forgiven, but lack of punctuality never.

The most often heard word in Denmark is *tak* (thank you) and its variations. It is so often heard that the air is thick with *taks*. This is what the famous Danish writer Mogens Lind has to say about it:

Two words crop up a great deal in the Danish language. One is 'I' and the other 'Thank you'. People say: 'Thank you' when they get their ticket in a bus or a train. They say: 'Thank you' when they are given their change. When they buy anything in a shop they say 'Thank you' at least three times. Variations of 'Thank you' are 'Many thanks', 'Hearty thanks', and 'A thousand thanks'. The two latter are used more particularly if you really mean it.

When you are invited out to a Danish house you begin by saying: 'Thank you for inviting me' (as your host welcomes you to the table); go on to 'Thank you for the food' when dinner is over; departing, you mutter 'Thank you for this evening'; and at the next meeting rush out with 'Thank you for the last time we were together'. These thanks are usually accompanied by a prolonged and hearty handshake, which must in any case be given on arrival, on departure, and after dinner or any kind of meal.

Like all foreigners, I enjoyed a great deal of Danish hospitality, both in people's homes and in restaurants. I've been trying to sort out in my mind some invitations that struck me as particularly Danish, and here they are: a Sunday dinner at Holte, a luncheon in Copenhagen, and a coffee party in Guldbjerg.

The Sunday dinner was at the home of Jens Peter Jensen, then the editor-in-chief of *Børsen*, the Danish financial newspaper, who lives in Holte, an upper-class Copenhagen suburb. Sunday at Holte was much as it is at home. My host was working in the garden, Mrs Jensen was preparing the food, helped by her ravishingly pretty future daughter-in-law Hanna. The older boy, Uffe, handsome in his lieutenant's uniform (the Danes have compulsory military service), was lounging around with his younger brother Peter, aged seven.

The living-room was large and filled with colourful and comfortable furnishings. I remember especially the beautiful needlework made by Mrs Jensen – few women would have the patience to do such fine stitching for pillows, coffee cosies, and doilies. Most Danish homes settle for an alcove for dining on one side of the living room, and the table was charmingly set with candles, flowers, and colourful accessories. (Candles are lit whenever a guest comes into the house, whatever the time of day, perhaps the warmest touch of Denmark's hospitality.) Our dinner started with smørrebrød, which included an outstanding liver pâté. There are probably as many recipes for liver pâté as there are Danish cooks, and they are all good, though some are better than others. With the roast came a dish of creamed mushrooms, chanterelles that carried with them the sweet, wild flavour of the woods, and I've never forgotten their goodness.

In many ways, things were as they would be at home. With one notable exception: it was Mrs Jensen and her son's fiancée who did all the fetching and carrying.

The luncheon was a formal one, in the big and beautiful house of Mrs A. W. Nielsen, the wife of the director of the Carlsberg Breweries. According to the will of the founder of Carlsberg, the Carlsberg Foundation is now the sole owner of these enormous breweries, the profits of which are dedicated to the sciences, the arts, and the humanities. These range from the Carlsberg Glyptotek in Copenhagen, one of Europe's great collections of classical and modern art, the Royal Opera and Ballet, the Institute of Biology, and the Museum of National History at Frederiksborg Palace to the restoration of the Knight's Hall at Kronborg (Hamlet's Castle).

Mrs Nielsen's table was exquisitely set in pink. The food was as beautiful to look at as good to eat. I remember the tiny shrimps, the *kylling à la king** served with saffron rice, and the most satiny custard I ever ate. The service was as exquisite. Mrs Nielsen, I was told, has the best-trained maids in Copenhagen, young and pretty girls, in their striped day uniforms, dropping curtsies to the guests. At Mrs Nielsen's table I saw my first Flor Danica china, decorated with Denmark's wild plants and flowers painted by hand on white backgrounds with the same skill and feeling that went into Audubon's drawings. The original service was created towards the end of the eighteenth century, Europe's golden age of porcelain, and was intended as a present from the Danish court to the Empress Catherine II of Russia. The Empress died before the set was finished, but over fifteen hundred pieces of the original set survive in the museum at Rosenborg Castle, an incredible assembly of plates and dishes, mighty ladles, knife, fork, and spoon handles, fish drainers, tureens and ice dishes, wine-coolers, salt cellars and serving-dishes, with gilded and crenelated lacy borders, a rococo fantasy ravishing beyond description. Flor Danica is still made by hand, as beautiful as the original pieces, by the Royal Copenhagen Manufactory, for those who can afford it. It is worth its price.

In Guldbjerg, a small village on the island of Funen, my hostess was the wife of the manager of the cooperative village store, which looked much like a store in a small English town. Mrs Rasmussen had invited a number of farm wives to meet me around the coffee table. The setting looked as pretty as a picture: the cloth was a deep blue one, red napkins peered from blue and white china, and small red flower pots held lighted candles among a trailing arrangement of ferns and carnations ranging from pale pink to deep red. No less than four kinds of cookies surrounded a golden sponge cake put together with layers of whipped cream, artfully swirled, a chocolate jelly roll, a fine *sandkage*, and a meringue torte. To sustain life further, Mrs Anna Thompsen, the best baker in the village, who had produced all this bonanza, handed pastry horns as light as snow-flakes, small and tender buns filled with home-made sausage meat, and more cookies. The coffee was plentiful, hot, and strong.

Skaal and Skaal Again

With the exception of beer, the Danes ordinarily drink only when they eat. That is, if they are behaving in a traditional manner, though more and more of them, especially in Copenhagen, are adopting the American and English cocktail and highball habits. A Danish dinner-party will be preceded by a glass of very good sherry, and wine will be served throughout the meal, with brandy and liqueurs to follow. The wine drunk in Denmark is excellent, as testified to by the wine lists in the restaurants and the care with which people choose it. Since grapes won't grow this far north, all of it is imported. The Danes favour French red wines, especially the Bordeaux wines like Médoc and St Émilion; in the Bordeaux region there are quite a number of shippers of Danish origin. Among the white wines, the Danes favour those from the Rhine and Moselle, but their preference is for the red.

The after-dinner brandy and the liqueurs, too, are tops, and the Danes also drink at this time sweet sherries, port, and madeira, all excellent. To a foreigner it is surprising to see how much the Danes know about ports, sherries, and madeiras, both for drinking and for cooking. For instance, I was once served a very fine vintage port at a remote and rather primitive farm. Though there are a number of local fruit cordials and fruit wines, the only one that has achieved world-wide fame is Cherry Heering, a dark red, luscious spirit.

The national drinks, however, are akvavit and beer. The former is drunk with smørrebrød only, with one exception: it is served with *gule aerter*,* the yellow pea soup that is a national dish. Beer, on the other hand, mostly lager, but also of all the varieties produced by the two cornerstones of Danish brewing, Carlsberg and Tuborg, is drunk all the time. Male and female, young and old, the Danes drink beer because they're thirsty, or because they're sitting down waiting for a friend, or because they're eating smørrebrød, or because the weather is warm or cold or windy, or just because they feel like it. (Thus spoke a Dane.) The foreigner falls in with their habits with no trouble at all.

Sweden and Norway have stringent liquor laws, dictated by temperance and religious movements. This is not so in Denmark, where by going from one place to another you can tipple the clock around, as the Swedes and Norwegians know; they nip across the Kattegat as often as they can. Yet thanks to the law-abidingness of the Danes, one sees few, if any, public staggers. The official attitude to drunkenness is also there, scaring off the prospective sinner. Danes who think nothing of zipping along in their cars at a cool seventy or eighty or more miles will say 'No, no, no' when you offer them a second drink before dinner. When you point out that they can't possibly get under the weather on so little, they'll explain with a sickly smile that should there be an accident, however slight, however much no fault of their own, they'll be punished automatically if the alcohol detecting test they have to take shows more than the bare legal minimum of alcohol in their blood. Another encouragement towards the straight and narrow is the habit the Danish papers have of publishing the names of people convicted for drunkenness. This is not a good thing for the offenders, not at all.

When the Danes drink at the table they follow a ritual. They take their drinks, with the exception of beer, in toasts, saying 'Skaal'. This does not at all slow up the intake, it only makes it prettier and more sociable. Foreigners are expected to fall in with the ritual, at least at the beginning. Here goes:

As you sit at the table to which your host has welcomed you in just these words, he will fill your akvavit or wine glass if it has not already been filled. Meantime, in the maelstrom of conversation, you listen for the word 'Skaal', the magic word. Your host will say it to you before anybody else. Watch him closely, and do as he does. Raise your glass to the lips, look deep into the other's eyes before taking a sip, toss down the potion, or sip it, look into the eyes again at lip level, put down the glass and, if you're drinking akvavit, reach gratefully for your cool beer.

The good host skaals each guest in turn. The guest, on the

other hand, should not try surreptitiously to sneak another drink from the glass that always seems to be full. He should take the initiative, fix his host or fellow guests with a purposeful glance, say 'Skaal', raise his glass, etc., etc. Husbands must skaal their wives, and they do so handsomely, even when a couple dines alone. Ladies skaal each other. The only person the guest must not skaal is the hostess. Somebody, after all, has to remain in control. And you don't skaal with beer.

As for the advantages of being not only allowed but expected to gaze deeply into the handsome eyes of a male or female Dane, they are not to be underestimated.

How to Freeze a Bottle of Akvavit into a Block of Ice

Akvavit must be served ice cold, but ice must never touch the actual drink if you want to do things in the Danish manner. The simplest way of chilling a bottle of akvavit is to stand it in the refrigerator for two or more days.

In restaurants, akvavit is served encased in a block of ice. This is achieved by standing the bottle in a special square mould, filling the mould with water, and freezing the whole thing. But these moulds are not available to private citizens. However, all is not lost, and a perfectly adequate frozen bottle of akvavit can be achieved with a large tin and a deep freezer.

The tin needed should be about 8 inches tall and about 3 inches larger in diameter than the akvavit bottle. First, freeze about 1 inch water in the bottom of the tin. Then place the akvavit bottle in the centre of the ice at the bottom of the tin. Add cold water almost to reach the top. Place the tin in the freezer and make sure the bottle remains dead centre.

When the water around the bottle is frozen solid, dip the tin quickly into hot water. The bottle in its ice coating is then easily removed. Serve the akvavit by holding the bottle in a napkin.

The Pleasure of Danish Restaurants

The Danes dine out a great deal, and they also take their guests to restaurants. But when the Danes dine out they don't want to find home cooking. They go to feast.

A meal in a good Danish restaurant is a revelation for English people. The table settings include a wealth of beautiful flowers, the kind you see in the shops of luxury florists at home. The service is fabulous, though the Danes say in a muted manner that things are not what they used to be. The waiters know English and advise you with tender care on the respective merits of an appetizer called 'a little tidbit' which consists of *pâté de foie gras* on dressed lettuce, with a tomato filled with port wine jelly or a *homard Rothschild* of lobster and mushrooms served in the shell in *sauce américaine*, flavoured with sherry, cognac, and paprika, glazed. (These are two specialities from the Belle Terrasse in Copenhagen, a restaurant that can only be called a bower of the most exquisite flowers which are matched by beautiful food.)

The menu cards and wine lists are of a length and magnitude that leave most visitors in a dazed state. Very often the dishes are explained in English, and even illustrated in colour in a thoughtful manner. You'll have to decide whether you want a fillet of sole Lucullus with mussels, fresh smoked salmon, asparagus, creamed mushrooms, lobster, shrimp, rice pilaff, and hollandaise sauce, or a saddle of venison with fruit jelly, cranberries, Waldorf salad, *pommes rissolées*, and cream sauce. This could be followed perhaps by a Cleopatra dessert: a chocolate basket filled with pistachio and vanilla ice cream, pineapple, whipped cream, and crystallized violets; or a Butterfly concoction of fancy ice creams with chocolate and fruits, served with fireworks. (These from the Seven Small Homes in Copenhagen, which has seven differently furnished rooms, all charming.)

At the restaurant of the Hotel d'Angleterre in Copenhagen

your luncheon omelet will come with diced potatoes, asparagus, tomato, bacon, radishes, shrimps, lettuce, and chives and look like spring on a plate. And if you want pancakes, they'll be stuffed with chopped raisins, soaked in black-currant rum, and flamed.

The food is served with elegance and verve. Since the portions are enormous, and far more than an average English person can eat, the food is kept hot on hot plates for second and third helpings, and if you give up before everything is gone the waiter, the maître, and the owner will be genuinely distressed and want to give you something else you might like better. Naturally, the food is served at the table from serving dishes. A few restaurants have introduced 'plate service', but restaurateurs are ashamed of this, because they feel that the food gets cold and that it is not possible to create a beautiful picture with it.

There's another festive note to Danish restaurant dining, and that's the music. Most restaurants have a trio or quartet of professional musicians playing gentle, semi-classical tunes during dinner. One feels relaxed and opulent, what with the handsome food, the solicitous waiters, the soft music, and the Danish eyes to gaze into while skaaling. And in many restaurants you can dance, because the Danes of all ages love to dance, all night.

Apart from the city restaurants, throughout Denmark there are the *kroer*, the country inns, some very old, some very modern, some for the family, and some for sophisticates. One of the most pleasant is the old rambling Rødvig Kro in a small fishing village by the gently lapping waves of the Baltic, which has been in the same family for well over a hundred years. The fishermen have their own wood-panelled parlour, the resident guests sit in two cosy rooms heated with charming old three-tier iron stoves, and across the road there is that other delightful Danish institution, the summer pavilion, where you dine and dance in the soft summer night among the Danish families and their polite, starched little boys and girls. In many of these inns you don't even have to order food to be welcomed. Signs proclaim that you can bring your own sandwiches; all that is expected of you is that you order a bottle of beer or a cup of coffee and ask for service. In return you'll be provided, free of charge, with a plate, silverware, and salt and pepper for your own food. If you order a piece of cake the owner will be more than happy.

No visitor to Denmark should miss a luncheon in a sandwich shop, where he'll find only the natives. Often these look like old-fashioned clubs. At Kronborg's in Copenhagen the foods are displayed on a counter and you select the makings of your smørrebrød, which will be brought to you, to be consumed with a *snaps* schnapps and a beer, or just a beer. Very Danish too are the wineshops, where you can also eat, and the *konditorier*, crowded at all times, where Danes and foreigners alike stuff themselves on rich and irresistible cakes buried under clouds of whipped cream. When the weather permits, the cafés and *konditorier* migrate to the pavements with their awnings and tables.

One phrase, in Danish, more than any other typifies Danish hospitality. You hear it all around you, as the waiter brings your food, or the waitress in a tiny country inn pours your coffee, or as your hostess welcomes you to the table. The phrase is '*Vaer saa god*,' which literally means, 'If you please.' *Vaer saa god* may be a standard phrase, but when you know the Danes, you know that it is said with sincerity, warming the cockles of a stranger's heart.

Where to Eat in Denmark

There are many fine restaurants in Denmark, most of them in Copenhagen, since it is the largest city. Foreigners might not hear of them, and never venture beyond the excellent dining-rooms of their hotels. For the sake of variety, the traveller should ask his hotel concierge or local people where the Danes go when they want to eat well. He will find the information worth while.

One thing must be remembered. The best eating places in Denmark – and in all of Scandinavia – are respectable and often elegant establishments, often located in smart hotels. Bistro discovering, so dear to travellers in France and Italy, is no sport for the North. There are few, if any, clever little places to which the natives repair. The Northerners don't like obscurity, and when they eat out they want to do so in style.

All Danish hotels and restaurants are painstakingly clean and wholesome. They are reasonably priced and a twelve per cent service charge is added to the price. This service charge means what it says; the only people you need tip are those who have done some extra service for you beyond the call of duty. If you don't, they will still be polite.

You can live and eat for very little in the 'Mission Hotels', which have nothing to do with religion but are clean, comfortable, and unassuming hostelries.

Here follows a list of restaurants throughout Denmark. The list is by no means complete, and there are many more places where you will find good food. But it is at least a starter.

RESTAURANTS IN COPENHAGEN

In Hotels:

Hotel d'Angleterre, Kongens Nytorv 34
Hotel Nordland, Vesterbrogade 22
Hotel Richmond, Vester Farimagsgade 33
Palace Hotel, Raadhuspladsen 57
Plaza Hotel, Bernstorffsgade 4

Without Hotels:

The 7 Small Homes (7 *smaa Hjem*), Jernbanegade 4

Coq d'Or, H. C. Andersens Boulevard 13 (Danish food in the French manner)

Krogs Fiskerestaurant, Gammel Strand 38 (excellent fish)

Belle Terrasse, Tivoli (charming interior and surroundings)

Oskar Davidsen, Aaboulevard 56 (open-faced sandwiches are the speciality)

The following restaurants are listed because they are patronized by Danes (rather than foreigners), especially at noontime when they do not want a large meal. All are very good, but simpler than the places above, in their selection and presentation of the food.

Grøften, Tivoli (shrimp, Danish delight)

Axelborg Bodega, Axeltorv 1 (herring, cold cuts, Danish omelet)

Tokanten, Vandkunsten 1 (Bohemian atmosphere)
Nyhavns Faergekro, Nyhavn 5 (in the old port district)
Hviids Vinstue, Kongens Nytorv 19 (a wineshop)
A Porta, Kongens Nytorv 17 (with a large summer terrace)

The Kvindernes Alkoholfrie Restauranter, where no alcoholic beverages are served, the food is most reasonably priced, and the surroundings clean and pleasant. These are at:
Vesterbrogade 35
Frederiksberggade 24

RESTAURANTS OUTSIDE COPENHAGEN

AABENRAA
Hotel Søgaardhus, pr. Kliplev

AALBORG
Hotel Phønix, Vesterbro 77

AARHUS
Hotel Royal, Store Torv 4
Motel 'La Tour', Randersvej 139

AERØSKØBING
Hotel Harmonien, Brogade

ANS
Kongensbro Kro

CHRISTIANSFELD
'Hos Stricker', Lindegade 25

FEMMØLLER
Mols-Kroen

FREDENSBORG
Store Kro

FREDERICIA
Hotel Landsoldaten, Danmarksgade 2

HAARBY, Fyn
Haarby Kro

HELSINGØR (site of Hamlet's castle)
Marienlyst, Kur-og

HERNING
Hotel Eyde, Torvet

HORSENS
Bygholm Parkhotel

KARUP
Karup Hotel

KOLDING
Hotel Jydekroen, Gudsø pr. Eltang
Saxildhus Hotel, Jernbanegade 39

NAESTVED
Mogenstrup Kro
Hotel Vinhuset, Sct. Peders Kirkeplads 4

NAKSKOV
Hotel Harmonien, Nybrogade 2

ODENSE
Grand Hotel, Jernbanegade 18
Restaurant Bang, Vestergade
Restaurant Skoven
Den gamle Kro, Overgade 23

RANDERS (famous for salmon)
Hotel Randers

RIBE
Hotel Dagmar, Torvet

RØDVIG
Rødvig Kro

ROLD SKOV
Rold Storkro

RØNNE
Dans Hotel, Krystalgade

SILKEBORG
Hotel Dania

SKAGEN
Brøndum Hotel

SKANDERBORG
Skanderborghus

SNEKKERSTEN
Kystens Perle

SØNDENBORG
Teater Hotellet, Perlegade

SORØ
Hotel Postgaarden

SPENTRUP
Hvidsten Kro

SVEDNEBORG
Christiansminde

TØNDER
Hotel Tønderhus, Jomfrustien

VEJLE
Hotel Australia

There are now four Danish Food Centres in Britain at 2 Conduit Street, London W1, at Cross Street, Manchester 2, at 10 Stephenson Place, Birmingham, and at 48 St Vincent Street, Glasgow.

Index

More about Penguins

Penguinews, which appears every month, contains details of all the new books issued by Penguins as they are published. From time to time it is supplemented by *Penguins in Print*, which is a complete list of all available books published by Penguins. (There are well over four thousand of these.)

A specimen copy of *Penguinews* can be sent to you free on request. For a year's issues (including the complete lists) please send 30p if you live in the United Kingdom, or 60p if you live elsewhere. Just write to Dept EP, Penguin Books Ltd, Harmondsworth, Middlesex, enclosing a cheque or postal order, and your name will be added to the mailing list.

Note: *Penguinews* and *Penguins in Print* are not available in the U.S.A. or Canada

Also by Nika Hazelton:

The Continental Flavour

This book is a carefully chosen anthology of some of the best recipes in continental cookeıy.

Nika Hazelton has gathered a host of ideas from most of the countries of Europe – from the Balkans, Central Europe, the northern Slavic countries and Scandinavia as well as western Europe. The styles vary from the highest of *haute cuisine* to traditional peasant dishes. The origins of some are lost, although the recipes themselves have been known for centuries; others are the happy result of flashes of inspiration by individual cooks. A witty, informative preface introduces each category of food, and many of the individual recipes are preceded by a brief story giving the background of the dish or the reason for its inclusion.

a Penguin Handbook

Not for sale in U.S.A. or Canada